A Genius for Friendship

WILLIAM BELLOWS
OF GLOUCESTER
1873 to 1942

by
Grace Bellows

WILLIAM SESSIONS LIMITED
YORK, ENGLAND
1982

WILLIAM BELLOWS

Contents

Illustrations

Foreword

by

LORD BROCKWAY

William Bellows was a good man. A Quaker, he showed friendship to everyone. The story of his life is an inspiration to try to follow his example. But this book is of value for more even than that.

Grace Bellows must have written with friends in mind, but this life of her husband is well worth a wider public for its treasures of historical and literary value, not to mention the thrill of exciting adventures.

There are intimate portraits of Leo Tolstoy, Arnold Bennett, Stanley Baldwin, Edmund Gosse (particularly), Thomas Hardy and others. There is an extraordinary chapter on William Bellows' experiences at the Ministry of Information during World War One which every historian of that period, indeed every student of the conduct of government departments, should read.

There is the story of William Bellows' visit to Nazi Germany to enable Jewish Refugees to escape to Britain, America and Australia – a heroic achievement.

There is his success, when an Alderman at Gloucester, in saving the Haresfield Beacon in the Cotswolds for the Nation, for which I am personally grateful.

There is the sheer excitement of a journey to the Arctic and of climbing to and descending from the top of the Matterhorn amidst stormy conditions which made survival a miracle.

There are dangers when a widow writes the biography of her husband. She may become over-emotional or biased. Grace Bellows is neither. She writes as an objective observer. And, in fact, the greater part of the book is an autobiography rather than a biography, for fortunately William Bellows wrote in detail of his experiences, sometimes in homely style but rising to fine writing in his tribute to Edmund Gosse.

Thank you, Grace Bellows, for allowing us to share your knowledge of a noble man and for revealing his knowledge of men of history and of historical events themselves.

FENNER BROCKWAY

September 1982

A Genius for Friendship
The Life of William Bellows of Gloucester
1873 — 1942

THIS BOOK IS A RECORD rather than a biography – the Libraries are full of biographies, especially of men and women who for some reason or another have been in the public eye, for curiosity is roused in many who welcome the chance to peep behind the scenes, to pry into the private life of Lord So-and-So or Lady What's-her-name, secretly hoping for an element of sensation and even something shocking. No – this book is not about a life laid bare for the public to gaze upon, from whatever underlying motive, but rather is it intended to recall the life of one who, a Master Printer and blessed with a keen intellect, an ordered mind, and a passionate love for his fellow creatures, set out to make the very fullest use of this equipment, unsparingly and unflinchingly, in whatever direction a service had to be rendered. And last, but not least, is it to show a genius for friendship, both given and received.

This record will contain nothing of a sensational nature, save accounts of perilous escapes in the High Alps and elsewhere, which only fellow explorers and mountaineers would fully appreciate, and certainly it will contain a touch of romance, only sensational in that it came so late, crowning a full and useful life.

This record will contain much of William Bellows' own writing – extracts from letters and accounts of public work carried out in the purposeful, steady way so characteristic of the true mountaineer.

But this record will have utterly failed if it does not carry with it also the sense of an abiding trust in the value of human life which was to be derived from companionship with him.

So let the reader judge for himself if this is not just a simple tale of 'Love in Action', balanced with innate wisdom and a natural humility.

Author's Note

AS THE WRITER, or compiler, of this book, I have endeavoured to keep it as impersonal as possible, as the focus is obviously upon the *quality* of the life of William Bellows, and its effect upon others.

Nevertheless, special mention must be made to explain how it came to be written so long after his passing, and an opportunity to render thanks to the one who was responsible for its production – a friend of his from overseas.

I asked this American lady to write her own account of how she came to meet William, and the circumstances around that meeting, for all I knew was that her name appeared in the long list of William's correspondents. When she took the trouble to trace me a few years ago, having lost many of her papers meanwhile, we started a correspondence.

This is what Miss Helen Moore of Boston (now Mrs John Franklin Day) wrote in March 1981:

> In May 1937 my aunt Mrs. Frederick Huntington Briggs of Boston, Massachusetts, U.S.A., took me to London, England for the Coronation of King George and Queen Elizabeth.
>
> A friend of mine in New York had previously introduced us to a Mr. William Bellows of 'Tuffley Lawn' Gloucester: a Publisher in London and a Master Printer.
>
> Upon finding a note from Mr. Bellows on our arrival at the English Speaking Union, where we were staying, we invited him to have lunch with us. We found him to be an unusually friendly person, and extremely knowledgeable of the various aspects of American life.
>
> A few days later, he invited us to have lunch with him at the Mitre Hotel, Oxford. It was a beautiful spring day and we looked forward to seeing a little of the English countryside. During lunch he told us of his perilous experiences while mountain climbing in the Alps and his many trips to Austria. We realised that we were with a real

explorer and we revelled in his stories. After lunch he took us on a short tour of Oxford, as we had to get back to London for another engagement.

After the Coronation, we had to visit very close friends in Belgium, but on our return he had wanted to take us to Stratford-on-Avon to see a Shakespearian Play, also a short visit to 'Tuffley Lawn' and Gloucester Cathedral. He was deeply interested in the fact that we both were members of the Boston Shakespeare Club.

But alas! With deep regrets we were forced to leave for home as my aunt was not well. In time we received a letter saying that he had found the perfect woman to marry, and sent us an invitation. We were so very happy for we felt that deep inside he was a lonely man, and was searching for the perfect companion.

Now, some forty years since then, I have met that 'perfect wife' for him, and *she* took me to see 'Tuffley Lawn' and Gloucester Cathedral, and while there William's spirit was very close. I have had the pleasure too of reading some of his writings which contained the deep concern he had for all mankind, and the longing for universal peace.

Helen Moore Day

In time, as she said, Helen was able to come to England and for the first time we met and shared the wealth of records and letters in my possession regarding my husband. She and her nephew-librarian, who was with her, urged that something should be done to make this material available to others; the first idea was to hand it over to the Archives of Gloucester, and they were delighted with the offer. Before long it became apparent that the message which William's life conveyed was essentially a human one, and therefore that warm flesh should be made to cover the bare bones of historical fact. Hence this book, which has come through so easily, and with such love and co-operation of the many.

May it encourage its readers to look for and value the simplicity of goodness where it may be found in this day and age, when competition and self-advancement seem to hold such high importance in man's aspirations and endeavours, for such lives as these can never be in vain.

Grace Bellows

JOHN BELLOWS (1831-1902)
From the portrait painted by Percy Bigland in 1901 now in Gloucester Art Gallery

WILLIAM BELLOWS
Infancy and Adolescence

CHAPTER I

Father to Son

ALMOST ANY PICTURE can be greatly enhanced by a good background, for it gives it an extra dimension, helping the observer to a deeper understanding of the subject – and this is true of pictures from pen on paper or brush on canvas.

This opening chapter therefore will be devoted to a swiftly outlined account of the life and work of John Bellows whose influence upon his son William is plain to see. Sons do not always follow in their father's footsteps, though if they do it can be for various reasons: to carry on a name in a profession or business, sometimes by compulsion, and sometimes from the weakness of a need to imitate. But the best example of continuity of father to son is when like calls to like, and the flowering of the son's life in the shelter of the home is as natural as it is inevitable, emerging into life as an individual being.

To commemorate the 150th anniversary of John Bellows' birth in January 1831, the following account of his life and work appeared in a Gloucester newspaper:

> Bellows was not a native of Gloucester. He was born in Liskeard in Cornwall. His father, William Bellows, had married Hannah Strickland, the daughter of a Wesleyan Preacher, and joined the Society of Friends by convincement shortly after his marriage.
>
> William Bellows moved to Camborne and started a school there in 1841.

Then followed details of what led John Bellows to go to Gloucester (after being apprenticed to a printer in Camborne) and there setting up his own printing press in due course, in the City where he was to become such an outstanding personality, spending the rest of his life there:

Bellows, who built up a large and efficient business, used up-to-date machinery. His studies of philosophy, and friendship with Max Muller and Oliver Wendell Holmes were linked with a keen interest in Philology, fostered by his correspondence with Prince Lucien Bonaparte. A journey abroad in 1863 convinced him of the need for simply produced, easily handled dictionaries.

His first dictionaries were produced on strong thin paper made by a Scottish firm for the Confederates in the American Civil War.

The paper had to be delivered at Charleston, but never got there because of the effectiveness of the blockade by the Federal ships acting under the orders of Abraham Lincoln. Bellows got hold of the paper as a job lot.

Besides producing basic phrase books for missionaries working in countries like China and Japan, Bellows published in the early 1870's a highly successful French-English dictionary. This was dedicated to Prince Lucien Bonaparte. English-French and French-English words appeared on the same page. By 1873 the first edition was completely sold out and had to be followed by further editions.

As an active Quaker, John Bellows was led to various fields of service to relieve suffering, so the article continues:

In the Franco-Prussian War of 1870-71, he was one of 40 Quakers who undertook relief work in the field for the Friends' War Victims Fund, intended to help both French and German civilians.

He went to the Metz area and what he saw strengthened his hatred of war and its consequences.

He wrote, 'I see only the torment and sorrow and death it has everywhere left in its track – the poor miserable man shrieking, writhing in a pool of his own blood – the white haired old General at Gravelotts, bending with a broken heart over the grave of his child – the nailmaker's wife in the Thionville road, crying in a despair more bitter than death, as she turns her face to the wall when her son is mentioned, her only son, from whom she is never to hear one parting word, and never to receive even the most sombre souvenir'.

Some years later, in the early 1880's, again was John Bellows stirred to continue his rescue work, for travelling in Norway he became deeply concerned at the brutal treatment by the Imperial Russian government of the Dokhobortsi, a Russian sect who would not fight, and therefore refused military service.

This led him to a contact which was to play such an important part in the rest of his life:

> He visited Tolstoy, one of their sympathisers, and with another Quaker, J. J. Neave, he travelled through the Caucasus to find out exactly what was going on. He played a big part in enabling groups of the Dokhobortsi to go to Cyprus and Canada.

Another facet of John Bellows' interests was History and Archaeology:

> He wrote about monastic orders and the survival of Roman architecture in Britain as well as accounts of visits to the Forest of Dean, Llanthony Abbey and the Black Mountains.

> One of the most respected Quakers of his day, he probably acquired his keen interest in archaeology from the discovery of traces of the Roman City wall at Gloucester when excavations were made for new premises for his Works in 1873 in Eastgate, Gloucester.

> He saw firmly that relief work was not about numbers of bowls of soup or garments distributed, or houses rebuilt, or tons of seed, or acres of land reploughed. It was about a succession of contacts with people and the rebirth of personal hope in them.

In the following pages describing William Bellows' service for those who were persecuted, it will be seen what a very real reflection was there of the example set by his father, so many years before the World War of 1939, when the Nazi persecutions played such a big part towards the end of William's life.

The newspaper article concludes as follows:

Bellows, who married a Clitheroe surgeon's daughter in 1869, lived on till 1902. He was also an inventor of a calculator for rapidly working out wages, and of a device for converting metric figures into English equivalents.

In appearance Bellows did not change with the times. In old age he still wore the traditional Quaker dress of his youth, and continued the old practice of referring to people as 'thee' and 'thou' instead of 'you'. A strict teetotaller and vegetarian, he had four sons and six daughters.

To this account can be added that a delightful picture of the Bellows family life has been immortalised by the publication of letters written by John Bellows to his friend Oliver Wendell Holmes in America in a large volume compiled by his wife, and so entrancing were these letters that the late Lord Birkenhead included them in his book entitled *The Five Hundred Best English Letters*. A veritable man of letters was John Bellows in every sense of the word, for the story of his life is contained in the wealth of letters written and received from the many outstanding people he contacted. And this quality can surely be seen to be reflected in his son William's life, whose great gift for friendship was partly dependent on his ability to put himself on paper. There is an outstanding example of a letter from a Roumanian lady for whom he had done some service. Writing to congratulate William upon his forthcoming marriage, she writes 'I have learnt to know only too well through all those years *what* you are, and cannot consider otherwise but as very lucky the one who will share your life. I am glad to have your photo, I can now have a more precise idea of you as you are, though I can scarcely realize I have never met you, such a true friend you have been during all those years to me and mine. May God's blessing be always on you and your near and dear ones for all the good you have done to others'.

William's great gift was to *maintain* friendship, and this he did throughout a life that was full to overflowing – no one was forgotten, and though there had necessarily to be long gaps in correspondence or contacts, yet it would surely be resumed when

4

opportunity offered. In this connection, in the words of Dr. Philip Gosse (son of Sir Edmund Gosse):

> William had many loveable qualities, and not least of these was that of friendship. Friendship to him was something worth while, not to be left to chance as is so often the case. When he made a friend, he set himself to keep that friendship fresh and alive. Like so many busy men, he somehow found time to write other than business and duty letters, and if some old friend had not been seen or heard of for a while, W. B. would sit down and write him a nice long friendly letter full of news and anecdote, and which required, and generally got, a reply.

There was a strong resemblance too between William and his father in a ready response to the plight of the persecuted. This was a quality they shared, and in which they were both true Quakers, following a fine tradition of rescue work, now so well known to history.

CHAPTER II

Family and Education

IT WOULD BE IMPOSSIBLE to do justice to any story of the life which William Bellows left behind him, save by giving separate attention to each of the many facets through which he expressed himself and his character, and then it would be for the reader to do his own summing up and decide what could be learnt from such study. It would be surprising, therefore, if the conclusion of the majority were not just BALANCE, a quality which is the direct outcome of a true maturity of being – a quality which mankind is surely, consciously or unconsciously, striving to attain, albeit under different labels, whether political, intellectual or religious.

The beginning of this story therefore must be devoted to a more detailed description of the Bellows' family background and the nature of the 'soil' in which they were nurtured.

William was the second son, having an older brother Max, and a sister Marion who was the eldest girl. Then followed two more brothers and four sisters by name Jack, Philip, Hannah, Lucy, Kitty and Dorothy. There was another girl who died in infancy.

This was a closely knit family, not unusual in those days when parents seemed to take their responsibilities more seriously, expecting to be true guardians of their children in every sense of the word. In this case, those fortunate children greatly benefited from parents whose deeply rooted Quaker principles could not help but pass on its influence to all in their household. All this is so eloquently expressed in the many letters, which fortunately have been published in the Biography of John Bellows by his wife, and it is a matter of considerable amazement that amidst a life so full of travel and service at home and abroad (much of which was shared by his wife) that far from there being any sacrifice of the family interests, they should have been such outstandingly dedicated parents to their large family.

6

William, like each of the family therefore, had this wonderful start in his life and, most important, was able and wishful to make full use of it whilst remaining his own individual self.

His education was not a spectacular one, no great brilliance of academic achievement, but rather an ability, shown throughout his varied life, to make the very best use of every experience and opportunity that came his way. Later in life, he called it 'sucking the last drop from the orange'.

In his early years William shared a Tutor with his brother Max. These two were closely knit, being near of an age. Later, they both attended a school at Bussage, which stands high up above the Stroud Valley. They travelled there by the old Railcar which ran between Cheltenham, through Gloucester, to Chalford via Stroud. They would get out at Brimscombe and climb up the hill there to Bussage. Whether they made this journey every day or were perhaps weekly boarders is not clear, though in those days children in the country expected to walk several miles to and from school, and certainly this was safer then than it would be today, and doubtless children would derive great benefit from the regular exercise.

William's further education took him to study the elements of mechanical engineering under the guidance of James Tangye, eldest brother of the well known Birmingham Engineers, and who was then in retirement in his native land of Cornwall.

The next phase of study took him to Paris where he spent the following 12 months in intensive work at the Sorbonne University, which was to lay the foundation not only to a scholarly knowledge of the language, but also a great love of its literature. All this stood William in great stead when it fell to him to make revisions of his father's famous Pocket French Dictionary.

During his stay in Paris in the year 1892, his father wrote to him from Petersburg as follows:

> . . . *All* our talents, *all* our ignorances even, *all* our strength and *all* our weakness, in the Divine Hand can be worked up into usefulness exactly in proportion as we are obedient to that which the Holy Spirit shows us we ought to do and not do. A man can do *nothing* of himself, unless it be to shut his eyes to the light; yet with every conviction that God brings home to us, He gives us *as much power to*

7

obey as will carry us through that particular requirement. This
measure of power ('power belongeth unto God') is also
called 'the measure of faith' ('faith is the gift of God') and
the soul in at once closing with it, takes hold of that power
or faith, and by it is carried through. This is what is meant
by 'the obedience of faith'.

And then John Bellows typically concludes by giving a clearly
expressed example, so profound in its simplicity:

And now to take a very commonplace illustration; when
we would be carried along the street by a force superior to
our own, we grasp the bar of a passing tramcar, and in
grasping it, we take hold of a strength far beyond our own
– we share the power, so to say, that is to carry us on our
way. But if we hesitate and stand waiting *for a moment that
will require no effort on our part* – the car passes; only to
leave us losers of so much precious time, and with exactly
the same condition to fulfill again when next the car
passes. We must thus much 'Co-operate with God'.

Thus, to each of his nine children did John Bellows find the time
to write and counsel according to their needs, often in the midst of
exacting foreign travel, sometimes by horse-carriage in very rough
conditions, for instance, in Trans-Caucasia. It is therefore no wonder
that William can be said to have started out in life with wonderful
equipment for his own particular form of service. 'Education' covers
such a wide field of subjects and experiences, and is certainly far from
being confined to academic studies.

WILLIAM BELLOWS
Skating and Skiing

LEO TOLSTOY
From photo by his friend Vladimir Tchartkoff taken in 1908

CHAPTER III

Journey to Russia
Visiting Tolstoy in 1906

WILLIAM BELLOWS' involvement with Russia, with Tolstoy and with the rescue of the Doukhobors, was a direct heritage from his father whose great activity and interests in those directions have received considerable publicity in one way and another. John Bellows' deep friendship from 1892 onwards with Leo Tolstoy was fraught with a wide divergence of views, and many were their discussions, both verbal and by letter, on spiritual issues; but all the time a bond of mutual regard existed, expressed by Tolstoy thus – 'I feel unity with you', and again – 'How *glad* I am you came over. O, how glad I am of your visit'.

Here is an extract from a letter which John Bellows wrote in 1895 to an American Senator, which also includes reference to the plight of the Doukhobors:

> In Russia, a body of people (the Doukhobors) quite unconnected with the Friends, have lately refused to bear arms; but along with the belief that it is wrong for us to kill one another, they have adopted Count Tolstoy's teaching that *all* government is abhorrent to the spirit of Christianity; I had some little talk with Count Tolstoy when at Moscow on this point; but could find no common basis to argue from. He has an idea that civilization, which admits of so many existing evils, is itself the cause of evil, and so would do away with it. Of course he is inconsistent; just as a man would necessarily be who tried to do away with gravitation. Thus he resorts to the press constantly, to spread his opinions; but how he could have typefounding and papermaking, etc., etc., without even a very advanced stage of civilization, passes my comprehension. So with

9

money. He looks on it as inherently sinful, so has as little to do with it as possible; though here again, of course, he cannot get away from the thing, though he may from the name. A. W. visited him and I fear lost patience with his unpractical ideas. Yet behind and underneath all this there is something really good in him, and a sympathetic power which has a great reach over most of those who come in contact with him.

Seven years after his first acquaintance with Count Tolstoy John Bellows wrote to another friend in Philadelphia:

I have been unable to approve of some of Tolstoy's views of things he has written; and yet, in sitting down by his side I felt the same deep and precious unity of spirit with him which I experienced at our last visit. Grasping both my hands, he said 'I have *great* love for you', and he afterwards adverted to the broadness of mind which enables us to recognize the love of truth in those who may not be of the same mould of thought as ourselves. Count Tolstoy was earnest that we should leave no possible stone unturned on this errand. [By this errand, he meant freeing the Doukhobors from Russian persecution by making their emigration possible.]

Small wonder was it therefore that William answered this call and offered his services to accompany a large number of this community, first to Cyprus and later, with his sister Hannah, to establish them in Canada.

William himself has left no record of those missions, but there is a detailed account of a journey he undertook, again with his sister Hannah, to visit Count Tolstoy in October 1908. This, in the original manuscript, is safely deposited with other papers, in the Archives of Gloucester, for it has the additional interest that it was corrected by Countess Tolstoy, who made a few written alterations. Later, William included a more condensed account in a book printed privately for his friends, and which can be given here:

. . . my sister and I remember him at the time of our visit to Yasnaia Poliana, within a few days of his eightieth birthday. The

earnest, deep-set eyes reflect the noble sincerity
and loveableness of his nature. He is looking out
upon a troubled world. It is something to have
seen the man himself, to have looked upon those
features, to have heard his very voice, to have seen
the home and the surroundings in which his life
was lived. The following sketch gives but a faint
idea of the actual experience—one of those luminous peaks of memory which time cannot obscure.

There is some sadness in reading over these
notes, when one reflects that the Russia of Leo
Tolstoy was so soon to pass away in storm and
suffering. He himself died on November 7th,
1910 ; the Countess in 1919 ; their family was
dispersed by persecution and exile. But one
thing can be said with certainty : his work will not
die. He sleeps in the little woodland enclosure at
Yasnaia Poliana where he loved to play as a small
boy. One's prayer is that after his own long years
of conflict and his struggle to improve the life of
men, the tragedy which has overtaken his beloved
country may remain for him a tragedy unrevealed.

How typical of William Bellows that he felt moved to make the
following observation:

I would like to make a reference to the Countess.
I have read the literature and the ' revelations'
which have been circulated since her death. But
to me she remains what she was at the time of our
visit, a much-tried woman and devoted wife and
mother, overtaken by the fate of things and mis-
understood. Her conflict with her husband's
friend and chief disciple, Vladimir Tchertkoff,
over the Tolstoy diaries and literary rights, was a
cruel development to come upon her in her last
years, and it broke her down. By her nature and
by the facts and necessities of her life she could not

follow her husband into the lonely, dangerous by-
paths which he was called upon to tread and so
there came to them both the sorrow of unwilled
yet inevitable separation which was the final sorrow
of their lives.

These tender words may well give others the benefit of his own
deeper understanding of a relationship on which history could well
have passed a false judgment. He goes on:

The morning after our arrival our host said that
he would like to drive me over with him to Yasnaia
Poliana—some two or three miles away—where
he would be spending the greater part of the day.
The tarantass* was brought round, and we were
soon trotting down the slope and into the woods.
In former times this forest—which stretches like
a green belt from east to west for, I believe, five
hundred miles—served as a barrier to protect
Moscow and the north from the hordes on the
southern steppes. The village of Yasnaia Poliana
—the 'Sunny Clearing'—lies on the confines of
this forest. We soon came in view of it, a cluster
of cottages nestling on the slope a mile or so in
front of us. Apart from the charm of the country
through which we were passing, the drive was one
of the very deepest interest, because throughout I
had the pleasure of hearing our host speak of Leo
Tolstoy, whom he knows as very few have known
him. He sees him regularly every day; and I
naturally made good use of this opportunity for
learning as much about 'Leo Nicolaievitch' as
time and the bumpiness of the road would allow.
On the grass we passed a telega in which a woman
was driving. We stopped while an exchange of
words took place in Russian and then as we passed
on, I learnt that this was a lady who was formerly
the mistress of a Government school for noble
girls in Moscow, but who had given up her position

to adopt Tolstoyanism and the simple life of the countryside. Here she was, driving round in the primitive telega of the peasant, and making a little money by growing strawberries for the people.

And so William actually came to the Tolstoy Home, which was the object of the journey:

In another few minutes we had come to the two familiar towers of brick which form the entrance to the Tolstoy home. On one of these is a small notice, by the Countess, informing all men that no flowers are to be picked and no damage to be done. The necessity for this is increased by the fact that there is no gate, and we pass straight in between an avenue of trees planted by Tolstoy's great-grandfather. The drive has rather an unfinished look ; it might be the entrance to an English country farm. But the very *abandon* of these outward details at Yasnaia Poliana only gives them an added charm. Two or three large ponds on either side are to be seen through the trees as we pass up the drive, and presently a tennis-court appears, and then the house—an oblong white building, with a green roof and a verandah at one end—the whole at peace with the world and bathed in the delicious sunshine of this summer morning. A peasant comes forward and leads our tarantass into the yard. Close at hand are the trees which mark the spot where the old house stood in which Tolstoy was born (1828). Moujiks at work here, and beggars, come and go by the drive, and it is evident that the latter are easily attracted across to the estate as they wander along the highway from Toula. We saw one or two of these poor people sitting on the bench which surrounds a shady tree close to the front door ; and more than once during our visit we noticed some pitiful-looking wanderer in rags turn in here for charity.

How much can be read into these simple details which impressed themselves upon this traveller. William goes on:

> In the simple entrance hall, with its two book-cases filled with works in Russian, English, Bohemian, Bulgarian, and other tongues, one or two peasant women were passing to and fro—evidently busied with some household work ; while from upstairs came the frequent click of a typewriter, where a lady typist was busy transcribing manuscripts. In spite of his physical weakness at this time, Leo Tolstoy's vigour of mind remained most keen ; and I saw many notes written by him in bed from day to day—small scraps of paper in the well-known, scrawling hand—to be copied out by willing assistance in a room close by. I could have spent a very interesting time reading the titles of the books in this little hall—but presently X. came down to say that Countess Tolstoy would be glad if I would stay to lunch ; so we went upstairs to the dining-room—a large oblong apartment with white-washed walls, with three windows at each end, and two grand pianos near the entrance. On the further side there hangs a striking full-length painting by Répine, the leading Russian portrait-painter, of Tatiana Tolstoy standing against a wall, with her hands placed on the back of a chair : a very pleasing portrait. On either side are paintings of her father in his younger days, and also of her mother. At table, besides the Countess and the members of the family, were one or two Tolstoyans in blue blouses, including a young Russian writer, and the family doctor. While lunch was going on, the door opened and Count Tolstoy's sister (two years younger than himself) came in, wearing the dress of a Russian nun. She has a nice face, with a grave expression. She spoke to me in French ; but as to English, when I met

her at table she remarked :—'Tout ce que je peux
vous dire en Anglais, Monsieur, c'est : How do
you do!' She was obviously feeling very anxious
on account of her brother's state of health.

Then came the welcome moment for which William had for so
long waited:

Near the end of lunch a message came that
Count Tolstoy would like to see me ; so his eldest
son, Sergius (who remembers very vividly his
journey to Canada with the Dukhobors) led the
way through to his father's bedroom on the same
floor. We passed into a lobby from the landing,
and from that through the small apartment where
Tolstoy does his writing, and in which his bedroom
door was standing open. The bedroom itself was
in subdued light, as a sheet had been put over the
the two windows to keep out the brilliant sunshine.
He was lying in bed facing me as I entered the
room ; and still at some distance from him I
noticed a wonderful tenderness in his face, a
certain expression which conveyed the idea of
'lovingness'—and behind it that unconscious
supremacy which is so difficult to describe. For
me it was naturally an impressive experience to
walk into that simple bedroom and see the famous
features. My sister came over to visit him two
days later ; her impressions were the same as
mine, and we both felt that it was worth the long
journey to Russia, if only to walk into that little
room! I expected to find Tolstoy looking younger ;
his beard, now turning white, surprised me, but
we must remember that he is eighty. There was
great vigour, nevertheless, in his eyes—his deep-
sunk eyes—peering out under the shaggy eye-
brows. He gave me the sense that he was glad
that I had come to see him ; as if it was really
myself whom he desired to see ! He held out his

hand from bed and welcomed me in English, while I took a chair at his bedside. Remembering how weak he was, I said that if he would find it easier to talk French, I would speak that language, but with a smile, and humour in his voice, he said : 'I will go on in English till my vords are used up!' But he was too modest; his vocabulary was ample. He mentioned that he had been reading a very interesting book, a little work published in India, I think, in English—'The Sayings of Mahommed': he handed it to me, asking me to 'Read that one,' and I read it aloud to him ; a short story about one of Mahommed's disciples who did not eat water-melons from principle ; not because his master did not eat them, for he knew that he *did*, but only because he did not know whether, *when* his master ate them, he began by splitting them, cutting them, or breaking them, open ! Until he had further light on this detail, he felt that it would not be right for him even to touch water-melons ! I need hardly say that Tolstoy enjoyed the humour of the story. Here and there the English words had been pencilled out, and their Russian equivalents marked in above, in his own writing. On the title-page were some lines in Turkish. I asked him if he could understand them. He said that he could make out the letters, which he had learnt when a student at the University of Kazan, but he could not read them, as there were only two vowels (which he pronounced *voyyels*, although generally his English was excellent). The difficulty was to know which vowel belonged to which place ! The name of the Indian sender of the little volume was written on the title-page, and I felt that it would have been very pleasing to him if he could have only seen how much pleasure the book was giving. Tolstoy handed it to me again, and I read another of the sayings concerning a friend of Mahommed, who found his master in danger. He, the friend, told him that it would be well for Mahommed to trust in this case to his own sword, but the latter answered that an active belief and faith in the protection of God would be the wiser course : a moral which pleased Tolstoy very much. As I finished reading, he said, '*Is* that not nice ? It is *vairy* nice,' and said there was a probability of the book being printed in Russian. He remembered my father and his work, and spoke of him affectionately ; in fact all the family remembered him well, and Countess Tolstoy spoke to us more than once of him and of his visit to their Moscow home.

Mention was made of our voyage to Russia by the Baltic, and of our passing through the Kiel Canal, where we had been able to watch, from the deck, the women and children in their 'Sunday best,' and even to see mushrooms growing on the banks. On Kiel Bay we passed the German fleet of twenty-four warships—a mile of warships. 'Oh, that is terr'rible, terr'rible, is it not?' Tolstoy said with emphasis. 'They have a malady for those ships now. Even in Japan they have caught the malady. But they will get tired of it, you will see. I am an old man, but you are young. I shall not see it, but you will live to see how they will get tired of all that!' Whether the Great Powers *will* get tired of armaments during our life-time I cannot say : I fear the habit is too deeply rooted to pass away so soon—but there was something prophetic and arresting in the way these words were uttered, something which made them seem to me no ordinary words. Presently, extending his hand from his bed, he said 'Good-bye,' and I withdrew with his son Sergius. As I left, I expressed the hope that we should find that he was getting stronger again, but he said, 'It is the will of God ; I must obey the will of God in this, and

He may not mean me to get better.'

And so ended William Bellows' memorable meeting with Count Tolstoy, described in detail as befits such a unique event, the memory of which he was to carry fresh in his mind throughout his life. And to conclude this account, William adds:

> At the time of our visit he was within a fortnight of his eightieth birthday, and letters were coming in from his admirers in many lands. One of these, written by a young Japanese lady, gave him especial pleasure. It had been translated for her into Russian by a professor in the Far East. Tolstoy remarked that in distant Japan he was understood by this young lady, while some of those most close at hand were unable to comprehend him. Leo Nicolaievitch is not concerned that people shall follow the *letter* of his teaching ; only that they may realise in their lives the *spirit* of it by being true to the leading and dictates of their conscience. Thus, a young officer came to him in doubt as to his own position, and seeking advice as to his military life, and whether he should leave the army. Tolstoy told him that he could not advise him on that, only that in whatever step he took he should endeavour to be true to his inward spiritual guidance, a reply which is very like that of George Fox when he said to William Penn in reference to his sword : 'Wear it as long as thou canst.'

What a lot there is to learn from all truly great souls, a simplicity which ever rings true, and one is aware that bigotry and narrow-mindedness so often comes to light from their followers, who have not really understood their message, and therefore bring it down to their own level. This, as history repeats itself, has happened all down the ages, and for the purpose of this book it is interesting to note William Bellows' own observations, for another in his place would probably have made a very different story of a meeting with this great man. One of William's most endearing qualities was that in all he did and said he revealed his own intrinsic simplicity and directness of outlook.

S.S. MATADOR AT NEWCASTLE-UPON-TYNE

en route for Jan Mayen Island

JAN MAYEN ISLAND
Breille Tower on East Coast

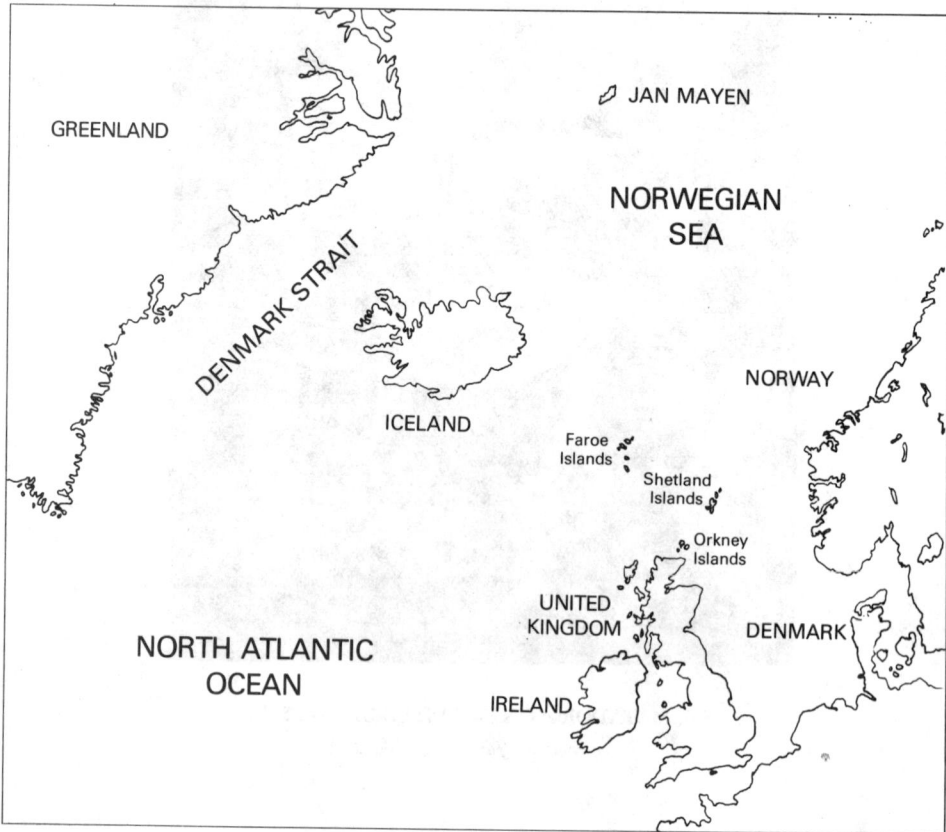

LOCATION OF JAN MAYEN ISLAND

CHAPTER IV

Arctic Adventures with International Flavour

IT IS, PERHAPS, a good thing that William Bellows did not leave a day-to-day diary – that is not to say that he did not share in full measure the family characteristic of recording experiences, often in print, and it was a gift that was to stand him in very good stead throughout his life. But if he had left a detailed and regular diary there might well have been the temptation to resort too closely to it, and thereby missing or confusing the very purpose of this book which is to explore each of the many facets of his life, giving as complete attention as possible to each, on its own merits; then it is to trace throughout an unbroken thread of purpose and behaviour which was his chief characteristic. It is so often one's experience in reading biographies to be faced with the fact that a man or woman, though standing high in the public regard for some particular and, may be, very noble service, yet when the private life is revealed it is a very different story, and one is left with a feeling of sorrow that it should be so. Whereas the story these pages have to tell is of a man who, wherever he went or whatever he set himself to do, could always be only and just himself. There was no need for the slightest degree of pretence or embellishment as he desired only to be accepted for what he was, and to be judged by those standards alone. Here follows an interesting extract from a reading of William's character by a qualified phrenologist which was obtained by a friend, without William's knowledge, and deduced from his handwriting. 'There is no assumption of superiority. He is nothing more nor less than he seems. There is no pose about him and no advertising. He hates flattery, show, ostentation and such like. There is some calm self-reliance, not over-confidence, just collected presence of mind. . . .'

In 1911, William with others, was thrilled to receive an invitation to join the Stackhouse Expedition to Jan Mayen. This is an island in the Arctic Sea, 300 miles north-east of Iceland, 650 to the west of the North Cape, 250 from the coast of Greenland. A cold lonely, uninhabited spot hardly visible on the map of Europe, and only to be approached in July and August; a cold, bleak, remote island of overpowering appeal to the lover of the little known.

This is the account William wrote of the expedition:

. . . The first thing to do was to find a suitable vessel. Our leader, J. Foster Stackhouse (who, later, to our common sorrow, went down on the 'Lusitania') searched the ports of Britain for a suitable craft. He thought he had discovered at Glasgow the very thing, but the owner imposed a difficult condition : the crew must be landed every Sunday morning to attend Divine service. But we were making for an uninhabited island where Nature herself would provide the only temple and Stackhouse, who could give no such Sunday morning guarantee, returned from Glasgow with a smile on his face but empty-handed.

At last news came that he had discovered, at Southampton, the exact vessel we needed for our purpose : the good little ship ' Matador ' with a crew of nine complete. The ' Matador,' all things considered, could surely not be improved upon and she was brought round to Newcastle and roped up to the quay below the Stephenson Bridge. With our bags and gear and tackle we bore down upon the vessel from our various points of origin : twelve from England, two from Sweden, three from Germany, two from America : indeed an international undertaking! The 'Matador' was a small steam-yacht of 240 tons only, with limited accommodation ; and there was an amused scramble for the best bunks and cabins. Those who failed in the scramble were consigned to a small place on deck where they put on bright faces and tightened up things to avoid being inundated with sea water. All looked well *as seen from the wharf :* the graceful craft lying at her moorings and the newspapermen coming on board to get a glimpse of, even an interview with, the intrepid navigators who might be seen thrusting up and down the narrow gang-ways with their outfit and personal bags and baggage. We had got into the ' Daily Mail ' and it seemed almost as if we were about to make history. At last the ropes were cast off and with the good wishes of such of the scientific world as lay within our reach, we glided away down the Tyne towards the grey, unresting sea.

Outside, the ocean wave proved unpleasant to the weaker links in our chain. Faces became paler and familiar figures disappeared into bunk or cabin. The ' Matador ' began to show us that she could roll ! Cold sea-water swept over the narrow decks and heroism took the form of sitting through the not too tempting meals. Groans were heard and the 'Matador's' timbers began to creak. We had brought with us a ship's doctor who soon got to work. He went round offering blue pills as a cer-tain cure for our troubles ; he did not explain that these evil things would make matters a thousand times worse. Then the rumour went round that so-and-so was suffering from appendicitis and that an operation at sea was impending. After a few anxious hours it was announced that so-and-so's trouble could not be appendicitis after all, as it was on the wrong side of his body. It must therefore be something else ! Yes, it was an unpleasant tossing—with the ' fiddles ' always in position to keep the uninviting food from rolling on to the cabin floor. Rocked on crest and buffeted in trough we presently came off the coast of Aberdeen-shire with the sea abating and a cheery sunny breeze raising the spirits of us all. Our route was to be *via* the Faroes and north-eastern Iceland to the island of our love. But now it became revealed to us that we had no bill of health on board and would be refused permission to land in Iceland or at any foreign port whatever! We would soon put that right, however! We would head for Kirkwall in the Orkneys and see the authorities. A regrettable loss of time, indeed, but an interesting one. As we landed on the wharf at Kirkwall we quickly found admirers among the crowd who looked on us as real Arctic explorers on our way to Northern triumphs: explorers 'of quality', to use the modern phrase. I remember with pleasure those few hours spent in the little Orkney town: the honest, light-haired people and the Scandinavian feeling in the air, and the various remains of past ages which we hastily visited. Then to sea again —every hour increasing the suspense and glamour and uncertainty of the coming days. At last through the gloom of the northern sea the great crags and precipices of the Faroes came into sight. We found our way through the foggy waters, past the huge rock walls with the tiny fishing villages at their feet. We sounded our hooter but not a note returned save the echo from those gigantic bastions. No wonder that William Morris was so impressed by the solemn, wondrous Faroes! Then out through a mighty portal into the ever-foggier ocean. Our next discovery was an unpleasant one. It became revealed to us that we had come to sea *without* a chronometer. What a subject for discussion in the deck-cabin, what a chance for each of us to show how much or how little we knew about navigation! We turned for help to the keystone of our scientific arch, Baron Klinckowström, of Stockholm. He explained to us the vital necessity of a chronometer; of all our sins of omission this would be our worst, our very worst. Never mind—we were not going to turn back, something would be *sure* to 'turn up' to save us yet! A bright idea struck someone; we would discover absolute time by taking the time by all our watches, pooling them, so to speak, and taking the average ! Then the fog, always lurking in these waters, began to thicken. The rolling sea kept the doctor's victims from stagnating, while the rest of us discussed the general scientific outlook from the crude comfort of the cabin, and by an effort talked knowledgeably of things we little understood.

Baron K. moved to and fro, looking very wise about these sea-matters and giving us his views. Thicker became the fog. We must be careful not to bump into Iceland ! Our skipper, Blanchard, who had never previously been further north than Cape Wrath, had a worrying time on the bridge. We were now off the most dangerous coast-line in Europe with nothing to cheer us but the long rolling sea, the darkening fog, no chronometer, and the ever-present suspicion of an impending ' bump.' What then was our feeling of exhilaration when suddenly high up in mid-air we descried in the fog-laden darkness the outline of the vast precipices guarding the entrance to Seydisfiord. Iceland at last ! Yes, here was Iceland ! Oh, to be in Iceland now that ice was there ! We drew nearer to the coast and ran in between the bleak mountains for ten miles to the little settlement of Seydisfiord, the third ' town ' in the island. It was streaming with rain as we disembarked. We were glad to stretch our legs once more. The fashionable wearing material at this place was black tarpaulin. Not a few only but *everyone*, down to the smallest creature, was wrapped up in his or her ' tarpaulin jacket ' The friendly, silent Icelanders stood there in the pouring rain, watching for the slightest sign of life on the ' Matador,'—in their eyes a ' hero-ship ' and nothing less. The rumour that we were bound for Jan Mayen passed round the wooden village and many kindnesses were shown to us. Chief

among these, I remember the hot steaming coffee
round a stove upstairs in a wooden house. Baron
Klinckowström was at home here. Dignified salu-
tations in Icelandic passed to and fro. Presently
the deluge ceased, the clouds cleared and the solemn
peaks and still waters of the fiord stood revealed.
We would take some ponies and gallop inland.
Already it seemed that Iceland was at our feet.
Fishing in the fiord went forward, and scrambles
on the mountain slopes, and above all a visit to the
lovely falls of the Fjardara coming down the valley
in glorious steps of purest water and sunlit spray.
How beautiful was the sub-arctic flora here—moist
and dripping with the mountain-mists ! The
little flowers among the rocks and by the streams
shone forth like gems of blue and pink and yellow.
And there were beds of moss of purest green,
bestrewed with diamonds of sparkling water.
Already we were forgetting the dangers, the real
dangers, of the work ahead. On the beach were
strong Icelandic girls, reserved and bonny, collect-
ing dried fish upon the rocks and stacking it like hay
in the watery sun. Some of us went inland to buy
fresh meat at a farm ; others fished in the fiord
and made a pile of slimy pollock on deck to gladden
the eyes of the ahungered voyagers. Our day or
two at Seydisfiord were quickly spent and with
many waved farewells and blasts from the steam
hooter, we put to sea again. The sky was clear
and the jagged lonely cliffs of Iceland—eternally
washed by the salt spray—stood out mile after mile
as we steamed northward. At one point indeed
we could see seventy miles of coast-line as if we
could reach it all with a walking-stick. Inland the
desolate mountains and northward the restless,
everlasting sea ! We were approaching the Arctic
circle. A few more leagues and we should merit
at last the glorious title of Arctic explorers. But

already fear was in the air. ' Berlin ' began to talk of our unpreparedness, of the certain risks of fog and of polar ice, of contact with the latter, and of a bee-line to the bottom of the sea. And then ' Stockholm ' joined the abdication party. We would go somewhere else ; Jan Mayen would surely keep and we could come again next year. Let us plan it all out again later on a *safer* basis ! Let our skipper take us back to the south and home. 'I tell you, Captain,' I could hear our Swedish friend saying, ' I tell you that if we do but meet with polar ice we shall be torn up like tissue paper —like *tissue* paper I say—we shall indeed perish *to a man*, my dear Blanchard.' The atmosphere was tense : for the British contingent (animated with the spirit of Captain Cook, of Scott and of Shackleton) was for continuing the voyage at all costs. The argument swayed to and fro ! The tension became worse and we finally decided to give up meals at the common table and to eat our ham and Dutch cheese at two sittings : the Southern party at one, and the Northern, or British, party at another. We British decided, in fact, that never again would we take part in an ' international ' expedition. Psychologically it was an interesting, indeed a dramatic, moment. Seas were coming on board and for a few unforgettable hours we lived through a dismally unpleasant time. In the narrow gangways and alleyways it was hardly possible to avoid meeting the men who disagreed with us, the Continental pioneers of ' Safety first.' Meanwhile, as the weather was getting worse, we decided to run for Cape Langanæs, the extreme N.E. point of Iceland. Here we should cross the Arctic circle. Fulmar petrels drove through the storm and flapped about in the air above our narrow deck. There can be few more desolate spots in Europe than Cape Langanæs. But is it in Europe ? Seen through the spray from our rolling craft it looked like the end of the world. Our spirits went down to zero. Through such weather and through these dangerous seas we could not drag half the expedition to a place it didn't want to go to ! For thirty hours we rode out the storm under the gaunt salt-washed cliffs of Langanæs. Fulmars, eider-ducks, and guillemots passed to and fro while we thought matters over on the comfortless ' Matador.' Jan Mayen or southward-bound again—this was now the question. The engine was giving trouble. We had been too much buffeted and a valve had given way. But one of the engineers of a British railway was on board : our good friend Angus. He worked all night at the erring spindle and announced at dawn that the mischief was repaired. The sea meanwhile had abated and our spirits rose again. The sun came out. The driving spray had cleared the air and the sea turned to a deep, almost un-imaginable indigo, and meanwhile our ' morale ' was rising. It was finally decided to continue our voyage. From Langanæs to Jan Mayen would mean thirty hours' steaming. If we could get there, well and good : if we could also return— *so much the better.* If our coal ran out we could hoist a sail : and as to a chronometer, well, we had our watches ! But now fog was coming on again and the temperature was dropping. Iceland had disappeared to the southward and there was ner-vous, concentrated talk of polar ice: polar ice which would quickly ' gobble up ' our little craft. It certainly became bitterly cold. That the ' Mata-dor,' designed for sunlight cruising in southern waters, was not suited for this work was obvious, by this time, to the most intrepid of us. Our coal supply was diminishing. We had been deceived as to the capacity of our bunkers and also it became revealed to us that the soft coal we had taken in at Seydisfiord was disappearing like a snow-wreath in the tropics. After all, the group which had been so strongly urging a very prompt return to our base, were wiser men than we gave them credit for. The long grey sea rolled on and we had now entered a world of intense solitude. Northward, steadily northward, the ' Matador ' throbbed its way. In the presence of the common danger and of the common thrill we all became friendly once again. Notes were compared, duties assigned for the conquest of Jan Mayen. This explorer would take over the fauna, that one the flora ; ' old man Parsons ' would keep us in fish with his rod and line. The Alpinists would tackle the virgin peak of Beerenberg (8,350 ft.) : Baron K. would act as a general lord of the manor, perhaps bringing down a bird or two with his well-polished rifle, or a fox or two. A pity that no one could secure a polar bear ' or two ' also, but they only come here in winter, crossing the drift ice from Greenland. There was indeed a prospect of plenty of work for each member of the Expedition. Then it became revealed to us that we must not tarry over-long, for our coal supply was diminishing *à vue d'œil*. The plucky old skipper was deeply interested in the proceedings but wore a slight frown. How would it all end ? Yes, indeed, *how ?* By this time the ' Matador ' must be somewhere in Jan Mayen waters. The fog was unpleasantly cold and it began to sleet. All eyes were strained in a N.N.E. direction. What if we shot past the island altogether and bumped into the North Pole ? Such a possibility was not to be thought of and the Baron brought up his most powerful glass—a glass which had a history and gave a scientific touch. Birds circled over head in the gloom and whisked past us on the deck. One could almost touch their pendent claws. Where did these birds come from ?

Surely from some northern terra firma ! We *must* be near the island now, for we had left the coast of Iceland quite thirty hours ago. We *would* see the southern rocks of Jan Mayen, we would *make* that telescope of the Baron do its duty ! At last it did. After a few hours of ever-increasing tension there came the cry of ' Land ahead ! ' Every glass of any pretension to transparency was brought to bear. A dozen eyes were glued on as many lenses. ' The southern rocks of Jan Mayen ' ? Yes, there they were at last, rising from the cold sea into the grey fog. The white breakers along the shore could almost now be heard, for we were fairly near in. This was a triumph of navigation under difficulties. All honour to our skipper Blanchard ! It was revealed to us that we had deviated very little from our true course. We were still a mile or so from shore but already we began to feel that we had Jan Mayen in our pocket. We set our course in a N.E. direction and passed off the Süd Cap of the Austrian Expedition (which came here in 1882), following the coast with care, for these were un-charted seas. In the enthusiasm for our approach-ing conquest, I think that some of us, myself included, entirely ignored the risks. The solemn coast-line with its steep walls of pitch-black lava, at the foot of which the sea was thundering in foaming breakers, made up an unforgettable pic-ture. We kept parallel with the coast for ten miles—treating it with full respect—and then cast anchor in Driftwood Bay, half a mile from shore. Here in the semi-shelter of the rocks we could stand with ease on deck again. Birds flew round us in excited, wondering flocks, skimming past us, soaring upward, returning at marvellous speed to the sea surface and off again. It was worth much discomfort and long leagues upon the water to witness this spectacle—bird life where man is

practically unknown, for this is a spot both uninhabited and rarely visited. When Dr Charcot
landed here many years before us he was met upon
the beach by two Arctic foxes who walked down to
salute him—no doubt the strangest animal they
had ever seen! As we lay at anchor our deck
was swept by a cold sleety wind and we put on our
warmest clothing. Equipment was dragged up
from the cabins and stacked in readiness on the
deck. Rifles, fishing gear, cameras, plant-presses,
and climbing kit! A boat was launched amid
wondering suspense : two seamen took the oars,
and Stackhouse and one or two of our co-heroes
took their places in the stern-sheets. We then
could see that the ocean was even less kind than we
had supposed. From time to time the little craft
was lost to view in the trough of the seas. With
anxious eyes we watched its halting progress.
Alas, the disappointment of our lives was in store
for us ; in fact was already at hand ! No amount of
wishing could get rid of the sinister reefs of black
lava and the wild lashing breakers which barred the
progress of the frail and tossing boat which was the
bearer of all our hopes. No amount of *wishing*
could prevent its being revealed to us that we had
chosen the wrong place for landing (they were *all*
wrong, as events proved to our undoing) and had
brought with us the wrong type of landing boat.
Oh, if we had but hoisted on to our decks one of
those excellent Faroese fishing-boats we had seen
further south : but further south was now four
hundred miles away. We heard later from members of what, by a euphemism, we will call ' the
landing-party,' that peering through the storm and
spray of the breakers there had been revealed to
them a line of sea-birds on the strand : a line of
birds some five or six miles long, holding possibly
their last parliament before rising for the south and

warmer seas. This vision of the assembled birds was to be our closest contact with the ornithology of Jan Mayen. The storm was not abating, and the spectre of that arch-demon, our lack of coal, was always hovering around us. The boom of the ocean and the cruelty of that coast-line combined to shake a nerve or two. Our little boat was returning : tossed up and down, now on crest, now in trough, it pulled towards us. At last we hoisted the ' landing party ' up on to the slippery deck once more. They had an unpleasant tale to tell us of things guessed at and even seen. To have come 1500 miles and to find oneself barred at last by those twenty yards of broken, tumbling water, this was too bitter even for an Arctic explorer. However, while there is coast-line there is hope, so we put on a good face, weighed anchor and continued a few more miles to the promontory of Egg Bluff. We hardly now dared to look at the stack of equipment on deck : it appeared to be taking on a visionary appearance, or at least to be losing its *raison-d'être*. We cautiously proceeded, here and there hugging the angry shore. We drew into the bay where the Nathorst Swedish expedition landed twelve years earlier : but it was the same story— breaking seas and a storm and spray-swept beach.

High above us rose the sinister crags and mountain slopes. To quote, in English, from the vivid account published by Baron Klinckowström at Stockholm : ' A wilder, more rugged scenery than that we now have before us is scarce possible to imagine. Everywhere dark lava-streams, craggy cinder-cones, slopes of volcanic sand or ashes, here and there patched with snow. We have just passed Egg Bluff, a huge sooty-black volcanic cone, or rather the half of a cone that, burst and cloven from top to foot by a last terrific eruption, is now standing with its opened insides like a sort of black and fantastic ruin. And everywhere, as soon as we come near the coast, the never-ceasing surf is roaring and foaming round the cliffs and along the beaches, driving any thought of landing out of our mind.'

Meanwhile we were approaching the *massif* of Mount Beerenberg, 8,350 ft.—perhaps the most northerly volcano in the world. Our eyes were directed upwards through the misty air to where the great peak should be. We were rewarded at last. To quote from the Baron again : 'For a short space of time the curtains of the fog fall again, and then the strong gust of wind sets them moving in the higher regions of the atmosphere; the cloudy veils of the mist whirl and wave, here and there specks of blue sky break through the grey fog and then, lo, now here, now yonder, like the wavering flames of a north light, dazzling, glittering masses of ice break through the clouds, the clouds that with every moment open more like the curtains of a theatre, disclosing high up in the sky over our heads a pyramid of dazzling snow, an arctic Fusijama standing out in clear-cut outlines against a dark blue sky. Ice-crowned Beerenberg, the royal, unconquered* and virgin, stands before us in all its wonderful glory' ! We had indeed been fortunate. It was worth making our 1500 mile voyage if only to enjoy that glorious spectacle. As we proceeded at half-speed along the coast, one by one the mighty glaciers of Petersen, Kjerulf and Weyprecht came into view, and we could see their ice-falls dipping into the ocean. High up on the slopes of Beerenberg a raging snow-storm was now at work. We took a due northerly course for the next ten miles, keeping parallel with the line of

* It was climbed for the first time in August, 1921, by J. M. Wordie and his companions of the Cambridge University Expedition to Jan Mayen. (See *The Times*, Sept. 21, 1921)

precipices, a thousand feet deep, which descend into the sea from the lower slopes of the great peak. It was approaching midnight as we reached the northern point of the island and our farthest north. The summit of Beerenberg was often in view as we steamed along : the moonlight was on the water, accompanying the last vestiges of daylight. In the presence of this majestic scene all our past difficulties and disappointments faded away. We could almost forget the ice-blink which now lighted up the northern horizon. But the captain, if no one else, could not forget the daily decreasing coal supply and we must not linger. We still had hopes of a landing-place on the western coast ; perhaps the sea would treat us more kindly there ! But the weather became worse and worse : there was not a bay nor inlet without its thundering breakers. What were the wild waves saying ? That we must hasten south at once ! We drew into Mary Muss Bay where we sounded our fog-horn for the benefit of any shipwrecked sailors possibly lurking there, for on shore there is a cabin at this point, stored with food. But no sign came from land except the evil flash of white foam on the beach, and with this there disappeared our last hope of landing on Jan Mayen. By 3 a.m. we had cleared the southern rocks again and the island disappeared once more into its solitude. We had failed in our object, but we had added a memorable experience to our lives. Away, then, in quickest time to the south ! It was time. On landing once more in Iceland it became revealed to us that we had just enough coal on board for *two hours'* steaming ! And as to the food served up in the cabin we were by this time absolutely weary of it. On our way south we put in at Faskrudsfiord on the East coast of Iceland, where we found ourselves enjoying one of the 232 days of fog which is the annual average allotted by Nature to that drip-dripping spot. Then southward-bound once more *via* the Faroes, to rope up again at our old quay-wall at Newcastle.

Sic transit gloria arctica !

EPILOGUE

At the time of our voyage Jan Mayen belonged to nobody. In May 1929 it was annexed by Norway. With this we do not quarrel, but what a chance we missed of raising the British flag on one of those cinder-cones, if not on the summit of the mighty Beerenberg itself! It is true that our party was an international one, but if matters had been put to a vote in the cabin, it is certain that the British Empire would have topped the poll.

May I add a few words about my late friend, Baron Klinckowström, the dominating figure of our ocean group. He passed away, alas, in the spring of 1936, leaving a very sorrowful blank in the lives of those who knew him. A man of many parts : a great zoologist, a great linguist, and a great traveller. A fine presence with a flowing beard *à la* W. G. Grace. He was educated at Goettingen University and had travelled both in the Arctic and the Antarctic. He became the foremost authority on the dachshund dog, but, as he said to me, ' after studying the dachshund for nine years I came to the conclusion that there were other things in life calling for my attention and so I took to writing opera.' He was the author of ' shilling shockers ' condemning Bolshevism and these had a great success in Sweden. He wrote a work on the ornithology of Scandinavia and also published the story of our Arctic failure under the title of ' With Britons and Teutons to Jan Mayen.' After our return from those wild waters, I began a correspondence with him which continued until his death ; his brilliant letters with their tang of laughing cynicism providing a literary feast of rare interest and humour.

As to our leader, J. Foster Stackhouse, he was last seen alive standing on the deck of the ' Lusitania.' A survivor of the disaster, who was talking to him when the torpedo struck the liner, wrote as follows :—' We heard a dull thud, and wreckage and water fell all around us. We all knew what it was and got life-belts, but Mr Stackhouse gave his to a little girl. Though he told me privately that we had no chance, he reassured many of the women who were breaking down. His calm courage and confidence went a long way towards stopping any panic, and in that way his assurance was of the greatest value in saving lives. As the ship went down, I saw Mr Stackhouse standing with his arms folded, perfectly calm, erect and smiling, without a lifebelt, on the boat-deck.' Another survivor wrote :—' The last I saw of him was on the upper deck, helping to push out a lifeboat which, owing to the list of the ship, was swinging in instead of out. He was begged by some friends to take a seat with them in it. He refused, saying : " There are others who must go first " and turned back to render further help.'

He had always hoped for a sudden death and that it might take place at sea.

CHAPTER V

Public Work in 1914 War

ONE OF THE OUTSTANDING experiences that fell to William Bellows' lot was the work he was invited to do during the first World War, and which resulted in some momentous friendships of life-long duration, and adding an enrichment of their own.

This work, since being a Quaker he could have nothing to do with fighting or armaments, was connected with the Department of Information in the Foreign Office (later becoming the Ministry of Information), for he did not scruple to help the cause in a constructive way by improving public morale in France. It can well be seen what good use his unusual command of the language, not to speak of his affinity with that country, were to the authorities, and not surprising therefore that he was rewarded a decoration by the French Government for his services in that Ministry.

This is how William wrote of his *Propaganda Memories*:

THE Great War, as we know, was not a war of armies only, but a war of entire nations : and long before the day of the final verdict in 1918, it was obvious that a *total* national effort and not any partial effort of the Allies, would be needed to carry us to victory: a concentration, in fact, of *all* our military, naval, economic, moral and intellectual resources. In this way it came to pass that the British Government added the weapon of propaganda to its armoury, just as it added tanks and paravanes in the military and naval spheres. This word *propaganda* was not a new one ; yet it was new to us in the sense in which we came to know it during the war. It might be defined as the official creation of public opinion in our favour, in the Allied and neutral countries of the world.

The Government department set up in the autumn of 1914 to undertake this task, aimed at embracing all civilized communities within its tentacles. The branch of the work with which I was associated and which I propose here to touch upon, related to France; the creation, in our favour, of public opinion across the Channel, the sustaining of French *moral* through the most trying hours of the war and the interpretation to the French democracy of the policy and intentions of Great Britain, their chief ally.

For 19 months William worked partly in the Department of Information of the Foreign Office and partly in the newly-created Ministry of Information. From Wellington House, Buckingham Gate, and subsequently Norfolk Street, the various departments controlled the national propaganda in France, Italy and the United States, Switzerland, Spain, Holland, Scandinavia, Greece and South America, the Far East and our various Colonies. Each of these countries needed its own special treatment, arising out of its particular needs. The daily press, lectures, special literature, wireless, the cinema, exhibitions, private agents and committees; those were the instruments with which the work was chiefly carried on.

Regarding France, his own particular care, William says:

... As to France, we had our national headquarters in Paris with committees at Lyons, Bordeaux and Marseilles : besides innumerable correspondents and agents dotted throughout the provinces. Our operations extended also to the French front, to the French troops at Salonica, and to the French colonies and spheres of influence in North Africa and elsewhere. We were frequently appealed to to extend our activities to the British front in France, but propaganda among our own nationals was no part of our task and was dealt with through other

channels such as the British War Aims Committee.
The Pyrenees, Brittany, the Riviera, the Vosges,
the valley of the Rhône, Paris, Normandy, Central
France, these consumed indeed all our energies !
The successes of our anti-submarine campaign, the
scale of our military operations, the work of English
women in the war, the problem of our coal supply,
the number of square miles of French soil recovered
by our troops, the work of our silent navy, the
sacrifices of the British taxpayer, these were some
of the many subjects which engaged our attention.
Every day fresh problems were presented as a
result of the progress of the great struggle.   Our
chief in the earlier days was Colonel John Buchan
(now Lord Tweedsmuir), and from the spring
of 1918 onwards, Lord Beaverbrook, a man of
discussable ideals and of great energy.   Twice a
week we met in private conclave under the chair-
manship of Mr Charles Masterman.   This propaganda committee concentrated round a single
table, so to speak, the public opinion of the world,
with its ebb and flow of pro-British or anti-British
feeling.   ' Charlie ' Masterman was a man whom
it was a pleasure to ' sit under,' whilst his gift of
lightning repartee made us look after our P's and
Q's.   To come under the sway of this ardent
Radical and ex-Cabinet Minister was at the outset
a somewhat moving experience.   The committee
was known as the ' Moot ' and questions of general
policy or of universal propaganda interest were
held over for consideration at its sittings.   In this
way during the discussions one came to estimate
the varying national view-points of distant lands.
Our Chairman had a fine gift for summarizing a
position in a few words, and an excellent memory.
From time to time when some urgent matter
required it, a special conference would be called
together, such as when the Germans were approach-

ing the Channel Ports in the spring of 1918, for it was necessary to be in constant touch with the official view of possible developments.

By the very nature of things, it is not easy to quote results of their propaganda which must necessarily be intangible. Across the Channel the supreme endeavour was to draw France and England closer together by every legitimate means, and it is doubtful if such a task had ever been attempted before on so great a scale. From the stand-point of the *effect* produced, there was, of course, nothing to rival the advances of the British Army on the Western front; what could appeal more deeply to the soul of the still unconvinced Frenchman than the news of so many square miles of soil, actually liberated by British arms. When such events took place it was their duty to make known the facts and carry the good news far and wide. William gives a description of some of the ways in which propaganda was used:

Special districts had their special needs. Brittany was considered, I think, our most difficult problem —with its clericalism and its ingrained anti-English prejudices. We worked upon the priests of Brittany —1400 of them—and tried to prove to them the sweet reasonableness of their secular enemy! Then there were the munition factories of Central France with their ' defeatism ' and end-the-war influences. In the Pyrenees and the South we had to combat the pro-German influences which trickled through from Spain. On the frontier of Savoy we paid our attentions to the stream of French refugees of sometimes 1000 per day, who were returning to their home-land from the devastated regions of the north. We prepared some special material for them and had thousands of patriotic cards distributed among the children. The Cunard Company in Paris were great and most acceptable distributing agents for our work, at their beautiful offices on the Bd. des Capucines.

Whenever one of our new publications appeared, a constant stream of visitors would call for copies. Their General Manager told me on one occasion that they had circulated a total of two million of our attractive publications from that office alone.

We worked in the friendliest co-operation with the British War Aims Committee—a member of which regularly attended our private conferences—and gave us much valuable help. For them I wrote a leaflet on '*France*' which was prepared for circulation on France's Day in this country. Half a million copies of it were nicely printed in two colours and circulated among the public. I saw it being distributed at Charing Cross station and was solemnly informed by the man in charge that 'that *that* one had been written by Monsieur *Cleemenceau*, and *this* one by Mr Lloyd George!' as he pointed with pride to a rival pile of propaganda literature. The article was translated into French and appeared in 'La Victoire,' on the 14th of July, 1918.

The propagation of British ideas abroad was a task so interesting that frequently it was felt to be reward in itself, quite apart from its effect as a war-time operation. This interest was undoubtedly very largely owing to the character of the men engaged on such work, and working in daily contact. Among the literary figures at the Ministry were Arnold Bennet, Major Reith ('Ian Hay'), Colonel John Buchan, Sir Henry Newbolt, William Archer and Hugh Walpole. No wonder that the Minister, Lord Beaverbrook, once announced that he was surrounded by *the* most brilliant staff of any Ministry in London. And to this list must be added the subject of this book! No wonder such announcement was listened to in respectful silence, without a word of dissent, for probably every Minister in the Cabinet knows the value of that kind of flattery!

Arnold Bennett began his career at the Ministry as Controller of French Propaganda and ended up as Director-General of the various services. William Bellows writes:

. . . My first acquaintance with

him dates from the 9th of May, 1918, on which day
I found him sitting at his desk in a carpetless
and barely furnished room looking out on to
Surrey Street. From this time forward as French
' National ' or executive officer it was my privilege
to work with him daily for several months. He
came to the work quite free from official prejudices,
of course, and this was of great advantage; although
even a genius can get his feet entangled in Government red tape. People used frequently to ask,
' Well, and how are you getting on with Arnold
Bennett ? ' ' All right, thank you,' I used to
answer ; 'I am in contact with a *live wire*, and we
are getting things done.' He suffered from an
impediment in his speech which from time to
time brought conversation to an awkward stand-
still. This had led him to write out his own notes
in shorthand, a process he used to recommend me
to follow as a great time-saver. His was a highly-
strung temperament, and I fear the strain on his
health was often heavy, and he would suffer from
insomnia. His great treat was to get away for the
week-end to his home at Thorpe-le-Soken in
Essex—there not to rest, however, but to work.
He told me once that after three hours' battling
with a new manuscript, he would end up so
exhausted that he would be fit for nothing the
following day. He was not often ruffled, as I saw
and knew him. He struck one as a man who had
tasted of all experience, and had very little further
to learn of life. I used to admire that fine forehead
of his and the attractive deep grey colouring of his
hair, as he sat with a huge fountain-pen in his
hand, drafting out some minute of his own, or
correcting, may be, one of mine. In the hot and
wearying days of summer he was anxious for me to
take over more of his own work; but of course there
was a difficulty in this which he could not see, the

inherent value of his own influence could not be replaced by that of a subordinate, however zealous. He could *talk* French, but did not care to write it. It was a happy appointment by which he was entrusted with the control of our work. For no one but a man saturated, as he was, with a knowledge of French life and character could possibly have carried on the task to which we were committed.

An interesting feature of the work of the Ministry of Information was that of bringing over prominent Frenchmen to visit this country, so that, with their own eyes, they might witness the huge effort of Great Britain during the war. There were many incidents, amusing and otherwise, in this connection, and to quote William again:

. . . I must mention no names but I remember on one occasion there arrived a leading French politician with his wife and private secretary. They were entertained by us at the Ritz. My colleague H. had them ' in tow.' I could not help thinking that there was something incongruous in seeing these people of socialistic views seated amidst the glittering dazzle of the Ritz. Monsieur was no doubt more at home than the others of his party ! Madame was glad to go out and look in at the shop-windows. This socialist leader was particularly anxious to get information on the food question and H. took him by appointment to see the Food Minister. Who was responsible for housing him at the Ritz, I do not know : but as H. pointed out, ' It would have been much better if we had put them up at some hotel, say, at Wolverhampton ! There, at any rate, they would have had real and unadulterated experience of our national food problem.'

An amusing incident occurred at a dinner given by the Alsace-Lorraine Society to honour a distinguished guest who had escaped from Alsace at the beginning of the war and was then serving in the

French Army. Following his speech which received a very warm welcome, was one by the president of some French Society who worked himself up into such a paroxysm of enthusiasm for the cause that he found it absolutely impossible to sit down again. If he was cheered to bring him to a close, he went on again with greater zest than ever; if there was a silence he took it simply as a sign that his audience was hanging on his words. There had to be a good deal of coat-tail pulling before he was prevailed upon to stop!

It was on this occasion, the Chair being occupied by Sir Edmund Gosse, that William had his first contact with one who was to be such a great influence on his life. So again, we turn to his own words describing those first impressions:

> The chair on this occasion was occupied by Edmund Gosse, whose address was delivered in the clear, choice English which made it such a pleasure to listen to him. I was introduced to him at the dinner, and subsequently came into contact with him in connection with our work. He took a great interest in the task which we had in hand, and I felt well pleased at having on one occasion, so to speak, roped him in for active help. He was a man whom it was necessary to *ménager*, as the French say. Highly-strung and not enjoying the best of health, he was not one 'to suffer fools gladly.' On one occasion he was wrathful with a French propagandist who had been delivering an address in London on the French part in the war, and for whom he had taken the chair. What vexed him so much was that the lecturer had arrived without having in any way prepared his subject. His remarks came forth undigested and never-ending, or, as Mr Gosse put it, like 'oil from the widow's cruse.' But the address, in reality so halting and so annoying to our great critic, made up quite a good article when printed in the 'Westminster Gazette.'
>
> As I have strayed a little already from the subject of propaganda, may I stray a little further to relate

something which greatly interested me when I heard it. Many years ago, *viz.*, in 1867, my Father compiled an outline dictionary for the use of missionaries, explorers and students of language. It contained an introduction by the late Professor Max Müller. I do not imagine that many copies were circulated, but one at any rate found its way into the library of the late Philip Gosse—whose son Edmund came upon it as quite a young man in search of knowledge. And this same son Edmund told me, sitting there over a cup of tea half a century later, that it was that book which gave him his first enthusiasm and thrill for the languages of the East.

Of the many interesting people William Bellows contacted during his time in the Ministry of Information mention must be made of Professor W. M. Dixon – afterwards back at his old post, the Chair of English Literature at Glasgow University. He succeeded Sir Gilbert Parker as chief officer in charge of the work in the United States. The extent of his operation was prodigious. His chief colleague and assistant was Professor Kemp-Smith, afterwards Professor of Logic at Edinburgh University. Those two men might be found facing one another for month after month at a large table in a quiet room at the Ministry. It was a treat to go into that room, especially at tea-time. Interesting though the work was it involved continuous strain, and so it was something to have a haven like Professor Dixon's to resort to, for a yawn and a cup of tea, and a comparing of notes on their common propaganda triumphs and tribulations. There were times when the latter seemed to choke the former, when they would gnash their teeth at the red tape and then settle down into a resigned laugh. Dixon had special knowledge about the work of the navy, and they circulated in France thousands of copies of a French translation of his 'British Navy in War-time'. On one occasion when he went off for a few days visit to the Grand Fleet, he received something of a shock and might not have come back to them again; for while he was quietly promenading the deck of a warship in the Firth of Forth, an urgent message was received to put to sea at once for the Germans were 'out'. One can imagine what his suspense must have been until it was ascertained that

43

the Germans had gone back 'in' again.

A familiar feature of the work, were the famous *minute-files* – budgets of documents dealing with questions of every description, and loaded up with answers from every source. These files would come in from every quarter and without ceasing. If with persevering effort all answers had been given and it was possible to breathe freely again, the chances were that a door would open and in would come a nice little girl in uniform with further minutes piled up to her chin, a fair number of which she would solemnly unload, and then resume her journey. These girls flitted like rays of sunshine across the business hours of the day. Besides their round of duty for the State, they were the means by which hot water was brought up from the lower regions for the making of afternoon tea; the famous afternoon tea of Government departments, which was supposed by readers of the *Daily Mail* to last from 3 p.m. to 5 p.m., or later.

But William can never let pass a criticism without a word to counteract the danger of it being taken as a generalisation:

A great deal is said in the Press about the inefficiency of Government departments and criticism of this kind is the favourite pastime of certain papers when there is nothing more urgent on hand. This is in a way quite natural, for we, as tax-payers, are anxious to learn that we are getting as much for our money as possible! It is an agreeable memory, and I like to put it on record, that although there may have been cases of inefficiency and a tendency to over-staffing, our Ministry was a very busy place indeed, where those directing operations felt the seriousness and urgency of the task and a full sense of their unceasing responsibilities. This was reflected in the daily lives of the secretaries, typists, messengers, and ' flappers in uniform ' without whose help we should have striven in vain. I shall never think of the old propaganda days without paying a silent tribute to the services of my own French secretary, a girl from Paris who took such a keen interest in her duties, and worked with such devotion that she became a veritable *sine qua non* in our French service till the end of the War.

Still on the subject of tea cups – at Wellington House, in the days of John Buchan, there and before the transfer to the Ministry of Information, a very nice and helpful tea club was run; a few gathering at 4.30 p.m. in a small room set apart for the purpose. Around the table they would compare notes on successes, if in good trim, or if tired, on their departmental grievances. It was felt to be a privilege to belong to such a circle. The most honoured figure in the group was Sir Anthony Hope Hawkins, who always sat at his one accustomed spot at a corner of the bare table, on which would lie the communal box of biscuits. Sir Anthony, older than most of them, would listen to the conversation of those poorer selves with an amused look, often intervening with a pungent comment. In William's words 'I remember complaining to him once of a certain well-known author who preached one thing and practised another! Had he read *The Times* on national economy, and had he seen the said author's new book on the War, with its many pages of plain paper, blank paper most wantonly wasted. "Yes", said Sir Anthony, "but it would have been *still more wasted* if he had made use of them" '.

One of William's pleasantest recollections of those days was that of Sir Anthony's kindly, most attractive personality; no more courteous or modest figure he felt could be found in the whole department. His work was of a special nature and was carried on in the quiet of a room, an ex-bedroom he called it, overlooking Buckingham Gate. The memory of his familiar handwriting and closely reasoned minutes still remain.

Of course, things did not always turn out according to plan, even in such a well run Ministry, and there was the unsolved mystery of the 'Flags for Lyons' which William recalls:

> . . . I was appealed to in the summer of 1918 to send out a large consignment of Union Jacks to be hoisted on the public buildings of Lyons on the 14th of July. There was a suspicion that the Americans were going to try their hand at this and we wanted to get

in first. I obtained the necessary material from the Office of Works and a very fine selection was forwarded *via* Le Havre. The master-flag of all was a huge affair for the roof of the Town Hall. All arrangements were made for a prompt delivery of the precious load. Urgent telegrams began to pass between our dept. and Lyons. Only three days to run and no news of the flags : then only two days and the messages became frantic. Then only one day and things became more frantic still. What had happened will remain one of the mysteries of history. *The flags did not arrive and never did arrive at Lyons !* . . . During the autumn of 1918 I received a message from Barcelona stating that a vast and mysterious collection of Union Jacks had just reached that city and that, pending further instructions, they had thought well to fly them from the public buildings !

William Bellows' views on the general use of propaganda are well worth recording, and no doubt those months he spent at the very heart of such practices were of lasting value to him in after life. He says:

I think we can take it that propaganda in some form will become more and more an institution in human affairs. The days of hole-and-corner diplomacy were supposed to have ended with the Great War. If this be true, they will need to be replaced by days of *knowledge* among the peoples of the world—knowledge of the great issues of the new international order. Propaganda, by which the view-point and intentions of a democracy can be made clear to sister nations, will be a very useful implement of civilization, if rightly used. Perhaps in this land of slow-dying prejudices we shall have to change its name, for to the sensitive ear it sounds unpleasantly sinister. It is so easy for a Government, having gathered the power of the press to its side for national purposes, to retain it at its side for its

46

own personal ends. In our work in France we had to steer clear of all debateable issues ; we could not interfere in politics or recommend the cutting of the Channel Tunnel, or the establishment of a tariff, nor even could we press for the creation of a League of Nations, the Clemenceau Government having its own views at that time on the subject. No risks could be taken with truth, our statements had always to be proveable and reliable. The tempting story of the German corpse factory was specially investigated for us and turned down as 'non proven.' But there were times when the enemy placed most useful ready-made material at our disposal. The Lichnowsky and, later, the Mühlen revelations were no sooner published than they were exploited by us in every possible way. Our aim was to edit these documents in simple style for the multitude. It was through our department that the Prime Minister's speeches on the War were officially translated in verbatim form.

No public work of any real importance can be undertaken without the risk and acceptance of criticism, and so this chapter in William's life will be concluded by quoting the following:

. . . The Consular services of France were at our side, and on many occasions we received valuable help from that quarter. Our then Consul-general at Lyons, Mr Vicars, was our most useful and ardent worker in provincial France. He had created a large organisation in his own area, which absorbed great quantities of literature. Of course we received many criticisms and complaints. As Lord Deaver-brook once said : ' You will get no thanks or gratitude ; but do not be disturbed by that.' My friend (now Sir) Eric Maclagan, Director of our Paris Bureau, used to say 'The worst of propaganda is that everyone thinks he knows how it ought to be carried on.' And so we would receive visits from diverse critics and friends of the Entente. Some of these would put forward useful suggestions ; others would talk as if the Treasury were non-existent, others again would solemnly urge us to take some action which, unknown to the outside world, we were already taking. France is a large country; *how* large, one came to realize more fully month by month, during the progress of our work. For even if we failed to achieve all that we set out to do, our object was to reach the whole of the population south of the firing line. Remembering the scale of our operations and the pertinacity with which they were carried on, I think we are justified in saying that the sum total of our influence across the Channel favourably affected the Allied cause and that our propaganda was not in vain.

WILLIAM BELLOWS AND THE MATTERHORN

THE SOLVAY HUT ON THE MATTERHORN

CHAPTER VI

Mountaineering in the High Alps

IT IS DOUBTFUL whether the story of William Bellows' usefulness to the community would have had anything like the same impact if he had not taken up serious mountaineering fairly late in life.

On first meeting him in middle life, the vivid impression was that of a mixture of extreme kindliness and equally extreme sensitivity.

It seemed impossible that such a man could successfully deal with the ups, and more often, the downs of public life and still triumph. But on further acquaintance, it was clear that the answer lay in his ability to throw himself heart and soul into the rigours and joys of winter sports and, in particular, climbing in the High Alps.

He was of course, fortunate in being able to run a thriving printing business meanwhile, because, not surprisingly, he had a loyal and devoted staff and there was mutual trust without which he could not have given such tireless service through the City Council and other bodies concerned with Gloucester and the Cotswolds, to many public affairs and their problems.

In earlier days he had partnered his brother Max, and together they ran the printing business after their father's death in 1902. It would have been easy under those circumstances to relieve each other for various activities by mutual consent, and doubtless this is what happened, otherwise how could William have been freed to undertake that very engrossing work in the Ministry of Information in the first World War? But later, Max left the business to live in London, and for 25 years or so William was entirely on his own. As his outside work did not seem to suffer, it must be emphasised that he rejoiced in a loyal and devoted staff that supported him throughout.

In William Bellows' own words, he restored himself in the higher reaches of the snow-clad heights – it was for him spiritual nourishment without which he could not function on the lower levels of life.

That he had a physique able to meet the many hazards of climbing was all part of his equipment for service in life, and he saw to it that there was no wastage, for all that he ingathered during those times in high altitudes was given out in full as his life in Gloucester demanded.

In 1926 William applied for Membership to the Alpine Club, but already he had a far from insignificant climbing record to his credit. The list started in 1895 with Mont Perdu in the Pyrenees, and was succeeded by no less than 21 different climbs up to 1926. Of these only a few were outstanding, but the sum total more than qualified him to be accepted into the fold of dedicated lovers of mountain climbing.

From then on, the summer expeditions became a very necessary part of his life – the more difficult the problems facing Gloucester City Council, the more exacting was the climbing he set himself, which seemed to provide a balance.

As it seems best to present to the reader William's own accounts of climbing unbroken, so as the more easily to convey the atmosphere which his own words can best express, to anyone to whom mountains and the fascination of their conquest does not appeal, the advice is to skip the rest of this chapter, for it is meant to arouse nostalgic memories in those who have possibly trodden these same paths in past youth, or, alternatively, to awaken enthusiasm in those who are still young and eager for conquest.

The following was written in Zermatt on 16th August, 1925:

ON the front wall of the Hôtel Monte Rosa at Zermatt is a bronze medallion portrait of Edward Whymper, set in a vertical slab of grey granite. It bears no date or inscription other than the simple name WHYMPER in unadorned lettering. This memorial plaque was unveiled at mid-day on Sunday, August 9, by General Bruce (President of the Alpine Club and leader of the Mt. Everest Expeditions, 1922 and 1924) in the presence of a large concourse of climbers, guides, visitors, photographers, peasants and children. The front of the hotel was decorated with flags which hung motionless in the brilliant sunlight of a perfect summer day. Through the kindness of Mr Sydney Spencer, Secretary of the Alpine Club, I was given a position in the reserved enclosure just facing the plaque, from which I was enabled to take photographs of the ceremony. Two speeches were made : one by General Bruce on behalf of the Alpine Club (the donors of the tablet) and

the other by Dr Dübi, the " grand old man " of the
Saas Fee Alps, who spoke as the representative of the
Swiss Alpine Club and as a personal friend of
Whymper. The company included Dr Seiler and
some twenty members of the Alpine Club and it is
certain that no one who was present on the occasion
of this unveiling will ever forget it. As the flag fell
in the presence of the silent crowd, the features of
Edward Whymper were revealed to us in the sunlit
bronze: somewhat stern features, no doubt, and just
omitting that touch of kindlier and more human
feeling which can be discovered in his earlier portraits. A man of great endeavour and superb will-
power, overshadowed by the memory of a tragedy!

It is just sixty years and one month ago since the
Matterhorn was first " conquered," and since young
Hadow, aged only nineteen, made that fatal slip on
the descent just below the summit, which turned a
triumph into a disaster. It is not necessary to climb
the mountain to examine the spot from which the
three Englishmen (Hudson, Lord Francis Douglas
and Hadow) and the great Michel Croz of Chamonix
slipped and fell 4,000 feet. From Zermatt, by means
of one or other of the large telescopes to be found in
the village street or in hotel gardens, one can sweep
the vertiginous slopes in detail and come very near
to the exact point where a single misplaced foot
meant such swift disaster to the four men. The
story is told in vivid detail in Whymper's " Scrambles
amongst the Alps "—a book which General Bruce
described in his unveiling address as perhaps the
greatest work on mountaineering ever written. There
were three survivors left to tell the story of the accident—Edward Whymper himself and the two Taug-
walders, father and son. I have a photograph of the
last-mentioned, Taugwalder the younger, who died
only two years ago at the age of 80, and whose simple
grave may be seen in the little burying-ground at
Zermatt. During his career he had climbed the
Matterhorn 125 times, which is probably a " world-
record." (Another of the Zermatt guides, Hermann
Perren, has been celebrating his 101st ascent during my
stay here at Zermatt this summer.) In his photograph,
Taugwalder the younger is seen with his rugged,
deeply furroughed features and bright small eyes as
of a wild animal looking straight into your face : this

51

untamed look seems still to say " Yes, I was there " !
I like looking at that portrait, filled as one is with
admiration for the man because he *was* there. I have
been climbing this week with sons of the great guide,
August Gentinetta, who accompanied Mummery on
the first ascent of the Matterhorn by the Zmutt-grad in
1879 : and from one or other of them I have learned
many things about the heroic and historic days of
Alpine climbing. Heinrich Gentinetta told me of
his father's admiration of the younger Taugwalder's
perfect mastery of rock-craft : " perfectly wonderful
upon rock, was he." I have at home a letter which
I greatly treasure : one written to me by the younger
Taugwalder, in an uncultured, mountain hand, in
which he tells me briefly of the historic climb on
July 14, 1865, and of his own long experience of the
Matterhorn. As to the elder Taugwalder, he died in
1888 at the Lac Noir and was buried in the old churchyard at Zermatt which in later days disappeared to
make room for the new church. On the wall of the
small Alpine museum in the village may be seen his
photograph : a composite one with the Matterhorn as
a background, and a poorly photographed old-fashioned figure with a beard : a Cornish local preacher, it
might be, standing on a glacier ! That is all that
remains to remind us of the father's features. No
one now survives of that party of seven who first
stood upon that " misty mountain top " sixty years
ago, but this bronze memorial will continue to remind
the passer-by of the name of Whymper—the first
conqueror of the great peak.

And what of the Matterhorn itself, vanquished yet
still mysterious ? I yesterday spent hours alone on
the rocks and snow fringing the foot of its north-
eastern spur. The sun was shining in a cloudless
sky and the more I gazed on its stupendous precipices
and on the marvellous glaciers and snowfields which
adorn its base, the deeper did the mystery become.
There is no real " conquering " of the Matterhorn.
One is in the presence of something too gloriously
eternal and impregnable for any " conquest " by man,
proud as we are of those who first reached its lonely
summit. I am not surprised that men like Guido
Rey—the great Italian climber and writer—should
look upon it as a thing divine. One gazes on it

in the still light of summer and in the changing light of stormy days and the mystery deepens. In its stupendous setting and proud loneliness—in the superb symmetry of its architecture—is it not the perfect type of what a mountain should be ? I like to think so.

As the technique of climbing becomes better understood and the eternal appeal of the great peaks spreads among the ever-widening circle of those who visit the Alps, it is likely that the Matterhorn will be climbed by a greater and greater number every year. Already during fine weather it daily attracts quite a little cluster of votaries who attack it by the N.E. ridge, or by the more difficult and arduous Italian route, or by the still more difficult and arduous Zmutt *arête*. The story of the climb has been often told, but while my memory is fresh I will relate my own impressions of the direct ascent from Zermatt by the Swiss *arête*. There are, I suggest, five classes of the Order of the Matterhorn ! To No. 1 belong the early pioneers— the first conquerors: the men who penetrated the veil. In No. 2 class I place the rare spirits who have struggled with the Furggen ridge and failed : in No. 3 the men who take the Zmutt or the Italian route from base to summit : No. 4 represents the group of the Swiss *arête*—whilst No. 5, the most numerous of all, includes those who reach the summit by any route you like, with the help of a good telescope !

With my guide Cæsar Petrig (the father, I later found, of nine children) and young Alexander Gentinetta (aged 17) I left Zermatt on Thursday afternoon, August 13th, for the first stage of the ascent. On such an occasion how difficult it is to get away ! At the last moment something is sure to turn up. Someone sees you leaving the hotel and wants a final word : or it may be well to cram some more fruit and chocolate into the already overburdened knapsacks : and then there is a final halt to check over the equipment before leaving the village. It is all there—down to the spare boot-laces and the coloured spectacles— and we are off. On a cloudless summer day the ascent to the Schwarzsee is a torrid grind indeed, and one is glad to rest in the shade of the scanty Arolla pines or to linger by the way and admire the superb views of the Lyskamm and the Breithorn as one rises higher and higher above the deep valley of the Visp. There is a sound which comes up here like music from far, far below : it is the eternal song of water, running water—invisible it may be, and far away. It is a song which brings a sense of peace, just as many other of the experiences of the climber do.

At the Schwarzsee, I was glad to rest in the shade while my companions went out upon the rocks to stretch the brand new 32-metre rope which they had brought with them. This rope had the red thread running through its length which is the well-known guarantee of the Alpine Club. Continuing our journey, with darkness settling on peak and glacier, we had reached by 9 p.m. the lower Matterhorn hut and adjacent Belvedere inn (10,820 ft.), perched on a rocky shoulder of the Hörnli under the very shadow of the first bastions of the citadel. A bed had been secured for me (by telephone !) from the Schwarzsee and I soon turned in, for the night was to be a short one. At 1.30 a.m. the signal came : the well-known knock which there is no evading, the knock one hears but does not want to hear. Looking out of the small window into the still night I found the young moon shining over Monte Rosa in a dark clear sky : " the floor of heaven " was sparkling with starlight which bathed the giant panorama of ice and snow with a luminous haze. I came downstairs to the little " Speisesaal " where our early meal was spread : one by one other climbers came in and rubbed their eyes and sat down, until I could count eleven. I kept my eyes open to see that there were not thirteen! It is rather a melancholy time, that quarter hour before the start ! One says but little on such occasions. We might all be potential heroes but as yet there is no hint either of heroism or of pleasure in the air. Everyone is tense and sleepy and slightly querulous, aware that a long effort is about to begin and given to little humour at this early hour. We might have been a group of condemned criminals on our execution night. There was one young woman among the sleep-heavy *coterie*. I fancy she must have been the one who, later in the day, held us up on the descent through getting " stuck " upon the rock-face, uncertain whether to descend or to go back to the summit ! She was, however, in the safe hands of two

54

knightly comrades who finally succeeded in coaxing her downwards.

Now and again a fresh pot of steaming coffee would appear. Now and again a guide would look in to see what progress his " victim " was making. At last we issued forth into the night and sorted ourselves out. There were Cæsar and Alexander (their very names seemed to spell victory from the start) with the rope uncoiled in the light of a lantern. Then one by one we " roped up " and at 2 a.m. disappeared into the dark shadow of the rocks. The little lanterns carried by the guides danced up and down and swayed to and fro, casting their illumination thinly before them and then became separated as one or other of us made better progress than the rest. I shall never forget those bright swaying points of light, those little shining eyes, dotted upward on the precipice, whose presence at this hour made itself felt rather than seen. We had not gone far before we crossed a patch of snow to the foot of a rock buttress where the real effort of the climb begins : upwards, upwards by the flickering lantern-light. Already we had reached what at lower levels would be described as a " mauvais pas " : a shadowy testing point to be carefully, very slowly negociated over smooth rock : a point no doubt where many a faint-hearted or faint-footed candidate for the Matterhorn has been tried in the balance, sorted out and returned in safety to the " base." This spot passed, one begins the long direct climb from here to the 'Shoulder' or ' Epaule,' up innumerable gulleys and small couloirs, past pinnacles, columns, and massive buttresses of gneiss, and across sinister snow-slopes graced with an ever-increasing downward curve which becomes fused into the whiteness of glaciers far below. We were now climbing on the left side of the great north-eastern spur, the route being identical with that followed by the Whymper party in 1865. As Whymper himself wrote in his excellent guide to Zermatt (1910) " In passing from the end of the Hörnli ridge on to the actual peak, the exact ledges are traversed over which I myself led on the first ascent."

The only sound to break the stillness was the well-remembered " clang " of the ice-axes upon rock :

the " tang " of steel upon stone, and the " crunch " of our boot-nails. Dawn broke in an orange sky and I agreed with the guide that we might put out the lantern, which had been casting its gentle flicker for two hours. However he could discover his way up with the aid of that frail little lantern passed my comprehension! There is a particular route, but it is broken at every step by new buttresses and walls of rock with intervening pinnacles and a complexity of descending couloirs. On the way up one faced the mountain all the time. Coming down again one was at one moment facing inward and the next moment with one's back to the rocks, every muscle coming into play until finally I felt as if I had been passed through a thrashing machine. From time to time we crossed a steep, hard snow-slope running down a long way. I had sent my ice-axe back to Zermatt from the lower hut : but the lack of it was made up for by Petrig keeping a tight rope which was paid out from behind by the vigilant Alexander. Now and again the silence would be broken in this fashion. " This is where Dr Moseley slipped " as we were mounting slab after slab on the Moseley Platte—where the famous accident of 1879 took place. " Last year another man came to grief just below here." Once or twice we came out on to the very ridge that runs up from the Zermatt side and occasionally one found oneself sitting astride of the *arête*, with one leg descending towards the Matterhorn glacier and the other towards the Furggen glacier. But for the most part the line of ascent lies just over to the left of the spiny ridge. We crossed a couloir. " Make haste here please : falling stones come down here— it is dangerous to linger." Fortunately for us the merry dance had not yet begun and we were able to slip across ' unobserved.' We presently came to and climbed over the ruins of the former Matterhorn hut (12,526 ft.) of which an engraving appears in Whymper's " Scrambles ": now represented by a few broken pieces of old timber protruding from a mass of snow and rock.

The " remplaçant " of the old hut is the new Solvay cabin (erected in 1916—the gift of Senator Solvay of Belgium) which we presently reached. It is placed in a niche at a height of 13,124 ft. and com-

mands a marvellous, plunging view : the erection of
it in such a position must have involved great per-
severance. Outside there is scarcely room to stand
on the ledge of snow—the back of the hut being
wedged into overhanging rocks. If you creep round
the end of it, you can look down through dizzy depths
to the Zmutt glacier lying far below in its peerless
beauty—with mighty precipices rising heavenward
above you. The hut itself was in a dismally dirty
condition and I was glad to hear that it was going to
be " inspected " on the following day. It is only
used for emergency purposes : no one is allowed to
sleep there except under stress of weather or in case
of accident. Leaving it behind us, or rather below
us, we rose from rock to rock, pulling, straining,
heaving—here a patch of snow, there some black ice
to beware of. We were approaching the " Shoulder,"
which is so well seen from Zermatt and on which
one bears over to the left by a somewhat easier gradi-
ent to the foot of the more precipitous rocks which
take you practically to the top. I did not find this
" Shoulder " at all easy. There was a treacherous
inclined plane of partially frozen snow here—hardly
deep enough to cut steps into and needing every
caution. Climbers above us on this slope seemed to
be stationary—they were in reality moving one step
at a time—proceeding with great deliberation and
anchoring to the all-too-scanty excrescences of rock
which showed themselves. This passage was bad
enough going up, but was worse coming down. There
was so little anchorage that it seemed that a slip
on the part of the guide would end in disaster. But
on such occasions the task of concentrating on the
next step keeps your mind occupied. From the
" Shoulder " we attacked the formidable rocks where
the fixed ropes are. These ropes—or $1\frac{1}{4}''$ hempen
cables—are held in position by iron grips embedded
in the rock. They run very steeply up the face of
the great slabs of gneiss at the points where there is
very scanty hand-hold. One needs every muscle of
one's arms to negociate these roped passages. A slip
would be unpleasant but not fatal, as the guide is
anchored high above you and pulls heavily on the
climbing rope. But it is not a pleasant feeling when
one of the longer cables begins to sway in the air—

especially if a wind is blowing. The voice of the guide takes on a sterner note here as he shouts his directions from above. One or two of these fixed ropes were badly frayed and perishing—needing renewal. I found the " pull up " over these rocks exhausting after the long and unrelenting effort from below. Finally we stood on the gentler incline of frozen snow leading to the summit. Across to the right, one or two hundred yards away, Cæsar pointed to the spot—the sinister spot—where the 1865 disaster took place. After a further pull of ten minutes we came at last to the summit. To borrow Leslie Stephen's phrase (used of the Weisshorn) it is a " firm and delicate edge " of very hard, crisp and corniced snow—slightly undulating and linking the Swiss with the Italian signal marks : a narrow, granulated ridge with an abyss on all sides. The actual form of this *arête* seems to vary over a course of years, as can be seen by comparing its present shape with that of Whymper's woodcut of 1874. Beneath it and practically invisible in the snow is the final wedge of gneiss (largely composed of talc and quartz, and bearing many traces of lightning shock) which forms the rocky culmination of the giant pyramid.

No words can describe the infinite splendour of the view from the summit. One is raised, as it were, into the upper air, with an abyss on either hand. No doubt on a calm day one would still hear the distant song of water coming from far away and far below, but now there was no sound except that of the cold breeze chipping against the frozen cornices of snow. The far-off, limitless horizon was softened by gentle banks of cloud and summer vapour, through which a thousand peaks rose heavenward into the crystalline blue. Of the mountains to be seen from where we stood balanced on the icy, glittering ridge these are some :—Mont Blanc (unmistakeable in the middle distance), the Grand Combin, the Jungfrau, Schreckhorn, Finsteraarhorn and Piz Bernina : the Meije (in Dauphiné), the Grand Paradis (the highest peak in Italy), the Grivola and Monte Viso; whilst near at hand, dazzling in the morning sunlight, Monte Rosa, the Lyskamm, Breithorn, Dent d'Hérens, Dent Blanche, Gabelhorn, Rothhorn, Weisshorn and the Mishabelhörner completed the wondrous panorama.

This was one of those superb mornings in the Alps when earth really seems to touch heaven itself : when every peak and snowfield and glacier unite to form a spectacle of unforgettable splendour. In the presence of such a scene one becomes silent.

For those who suffer from dizziness I do not recommend the summit of the Matterhorn. The plunging view down the precipices on the Italian side may be described as vertiginous. And when the eye finally comes to rest in the Val Tournanche far below, it discovers the little village of Breuil (from here almost seen in *plan*)—so famous in the history of the mountain—and the base of all the pioneer attacks from the Italian side. It is not the least wonderful experience of standing here that one can let one's vision *drop*, as it were, into such unplumbed depths. In another sense let those who suffer from dizziness come here and train themselves to look down and down, for given a good guide, a strong rope and sufficient practice, I imagine that even dizziness may be overcome in the end !

Perched upon the snow cornice and nestling as close to us as safety would permit, was an Alpine chough, which seemed to be saying : " Good morning ! Yes, isn't this a *grand* spot ! I know it well. But do please leave me some scraps : I am *so* hungry and have hardly had any breakfast." My remembrance of that glorious panorama as we stood there in the cold breeze, will always have as its counterpart the memory of that friendly, lonely chough* with its red legs poised on the crisp snow, its inquisitive eye turned in our direction and its yellow beak slightly tilted down towards the abyss. Apart from breakfast, it only seemed to lack one thing—a pair of spectacles ! I would like to see what that chough must often have seen—the Matterhorn *in plan*. It presents not a triangular but a beautifully formed quadrilateral figure the Swiss, Zmutt, Italian and Furggen ridges converging symmetrically from the base to unite in that short fine line which forms the

---

* I remember, many years ago, climbing Mont Perdu (10,995 ft.), the second peak of the Pyrenees. It stands in a desolate world of rock and snow. Just as I reached the summit with a companion and two guides, a butterfly flew just over our heads and wandered away into space !

summit. We are so accustomed to the sight of familiar peaks in elevation only that the view of them vertically from above would probably often cause us to revise our conception of these mountain masses. We remained on the top (14,781 ft.) from 9.30 till 10.15 a.m. A touch of mountain sickness made it desirable for me to eat nothing but a dried prune (dried in the sense that leather is dried), so I busied myself with taking photographs. I set the camera on the topmost ridge and stood against the cairn, with Mont Blanc and the blue sky for background, while one of our party " pressed the button." Alas, when the film was subsequently developed it was found to represent nothing but a *blank* ! Other subjects were more successful. My hands, touching the metal camera, became very cold and it took Cæsar some time, by dint of beating and rubbing, to bring them back to life again. We now prepared for the descent, which was to take us 7½ hours to the lower hut— exclusive of halts for rest and food. It had been our intention if possible to descend on the Italian side, in other words, to traverse the Matterhorn. We left the final decision open till we reached the top. It was then decided, in view of the bad conditions (with much new snow) on the Italian side and the comparative lateness of the hour, to return by the same route as that by which we had climbed.

Leaving the cairn and summit cornices behind us we came down the first—and easier—slopes to the top of the first rocks and engaged upon the ropes. The sustained and testing effort of the ascent was now to be counterbalanced by the tension and equally testing effort of a continuous and marvellous descent —seemingly a never-ending descent—with glaciers and deep-hidden valleys beneath our feet and the immaculate snows of Monte Rosa facing us through space. The fixed ropes—scorned no doubt by the super-expert—greatly aided the descent on to the Epaule. Clattering down the rock faces with Petrig paying out from above and Alexander pulling in from below, I covered this passage *au pas accéléré*. One does not stop to marvel at the scene as one descends the great slabs of gneiss still touched in places with black ice—the bane of the mountaineer. One is conscious of glorious precipices ending far below, and of

the slowly breaking panorama of the giants, but this is
no place for a halt; so steadily downward, downward,
clutching at this handhold, streching down to that
foothold, now turning with face to the rock, now re-
versing one's position and facing into space, now
balancing along a ridge of hard snow, then down over
the solid bastions, downward, downward. But did
we climb *all* this coming up, one asks oneself ? Yes—
there is but one route here and this is the way we
came : these are the very rocks and the very ledges
upon which we had groped our way by lanternlight,
by the light of dawn, and by the rays of the orange-
tinted sunrise. To many, the descent seems longer
and more exacting than the ascent. To me these rock
faces and broken buttresses seemed interminable. I
could not help admiring Alexander's skill (leading
downward) in his discovery of the right rock, of the
right foothold or ledge, when so little separated us
from impossibility. The slightest deviation and one
was up against an impassable passage, an abyss, or
difficulty not to be surmounted. Presently we came
to a niche where one could sit and contemplate and
eat and photograph. Within the range of two or
three yards of rope I could work my way on to the
projecting rocks and look down the immense slope—
so easily seen from Zermatt—which descends to the
Furggen glacier. At every point the Matterhorn
exacts respect. Not all of these stones were fast,
and one or two which gave a slight tilt as one placed
one's weight upon them left an unpleasant impression
on one's mind, causing one " furiously " to retreat.
We now gathered up our things and continued the
descent—my companions well-submerged beneath
the distended ruck-sacks. Conversation between
us was rather scanty. I could not easily follow
their low-voiced dialogue, interspersed with merry
bursts of laughter, and moreover I thought it just as
well, down these rocks, to confine myself to the
work in hand.

Out of the purest azure and as it were by magic,
massed clouds were now forming and rolling up from
Italy, silently invading the ridges and glaciers still
far below us and breaking into giant masses which
broke upon and enveloped the precipices of the Furggen *arête*. It was a glorious vision of how swiftly the

scene may change upon these heights. One has only
to read the classic accounts of climbing in the high
Alps to see how rapid may be the transition from the
most glorious conditions of weather to an awe-com-
pelling tempest. Fortunately for us the silent cloud
masses withdrew for a time to other heights and our
fine weather continued to the end.

By 7 p.m. we had reached the Belvedere once more,
and after a meal in the highly-spiced atmosphere of
the guide's quarters—Cæsar and Alexander returned
to Zermatt. Having been for fifteen hours " on the
move," I was glad to remain here for the night. The
" lendemain " being a fête day in the valley, no guides
would come up to undertake a climb and I had the
place practically to myself. I rose in the morning to
find the fine weather still continuing—the sun shining
in a cloudless sky upon a gorgeous scene. It seemed
as if I might *possess* the whole range of beauty from
Monte Rosa to the Weisshorn. There was a sheen
on the distant snow and a glitter at the points where
the great peaks touched the sky. I could now examine at close range the stupendous masses of the
Matterhorn precipices descending into the sunlight
of the snowfields and glaciers at their feet. I
scrambled on to a narrow ridge at the head of the
Matterhorn glacier and from here could peer up at
the icy slopes and rock bastions of the northern
face—or look across the abyss at the giant form
of the Dent Blanche. Far up above me I could
see the tiny framework of the Solvay hut—and
beyond that the awkward slope on the Epaule, and
the splendid rocks running up to the little white
patch where the summit comes into view.

It was good thus to fight the battle once again
from the comparative safety of these slopes. Our
day " aloft " had been an unforgettable one of perfect
weather, although the actual conditions on the
mountain were not good: the new snow upon the
ledges delaying our progress and making the ' going '
more difficult, especially on the upper rocks. In
mountaineering all is relative. (What a useful
word " relative " is !) Conditions are ever varying
in a world of infinite variety and one's own condition may vary with the mountains. What is a
difficult climb on one occasion may prove easier or

still more difficult on the next. But whatever the conditions, each completed climb is, like virtue, its own reward. This particular one was no exception to the rule. It was a perfect and unforgettable experience and my day upon those precipices, surrounded by scenery of such surpassing splendour, proved infinitely satisfying. Given the necessary reserve of nerve and muscle, something of a " head," and the fitting opportunity, let my reader go and do likewise. He will find the valley-mists of these difficult post-war days receding beneath his feet and giving place to a quite celestial vision which will stand out for the rest of his days as a luminous peak of memory. And as he stands at last upon the pure white summit of the mountain he will find the truth to be that the Matterhorn *has conquered him!*

CHAPTER VII

Further Climbing

IF THE READER has penetrated thus far and enjoyed, whether nostalgically or in interested anticipation, the excursions into mountain regions, he will not be dismayed to find two more chapters devoted to the same subject. And although both chapters are relating to the same region of Zermatt and the Matterhorn, they each have a very different aspect and focus in the telling.

William Bellows did not leave detailed accounts of his many other climbs, so it is to be concluded that he had a very special love and reverence for the Matterhorn, as so many other, and very famous, mountaineers had, and put their experiences on record.

In 1926 William wrote what he called 'A Day in the Val Tournanche', and here it is:

HAVING slept at the Schwarzsee above Zermatt, we rose before dawn and followed the Matterhorn track towards the Hörnli. Then diverging to the left on to the Furggen glacier, we gradually mounted its upper reaches—probing the snow with our ice-axes as we advanced step by step in the flickering light of the lanterns. Finally a rock climb brought us to the pure white ridge of the Furggenjoch (11,014 feet), from which we could sweep with our eyes the glorious southern precipices of the Matterhorn. The morning was already breaking in a greater and greater intensity of sunshine, whilst far to the south in a haze of bluish light we could see the Grand Paradis, the Grivola and the rest of that giant group. After a photographic halt on the *joch*, my friends came down with me to the safety of the first rocks in the Val Tournanche, and then returned with our guide to Zermatt : whilst, under a perfect sky, I continued my way down over snow and screes into the upper basin of the valley. From time to time the deafening roar of avalanches of rock or snow broke the morning

64

stillness on the Matterhorn ; but so vast is its southern face, so stupendous the scale of its bastions and couloirs, that no falling masses could anywhere be seen. The valley is guarded by a line of peaks forming a rocky wall of 12,000 feet (beginning with the Dent d'Hérens), along which filmy clouds hung motionless in the morning sunshine.

Steadily descending, I presently entered a wild sea of rocks which had been hurled from the precipices above : rocks as big as cottages or haystacks, lichen-covered, tossed in every direction. Awful must have been the thunder of these mighty fragments as one by one they came to rest on the valley floor—to rest, no doubt, for a thousand or ten thousand years. And in among them, smiling in their tenderness, were blue gentians, pinguiculas, forget-me-nots and saxifrages, responding to the pure air and to the limpid sunlit water of a thousand streamlets. From such a spot how could I tear myself away ? Every mat of flowers, every brilliant colour held me spell-bound in this perfect little corner of paradise at my feet, with the sullen, awful rock masses towering above. I lost my way, but what did that matter ? Descending by steep slopes of grey moraine and across torrents and over slabs and screes, I came at last to the open grassy plateau which dominates the scattered hamlet of Breuil.

First one comes to the " Grand Hotel Mont Cervin " at Giomein (we are here at 6,500 feet)—a large plain Italian building, offering as much comfort as is good for one. Below it in the valley lies the hamlet proper. My chief object in coming to Breuil was to visit Guido Rey, the great climber, writer, and lover of all mountains great and small. On the edge of the larchwoods, outside the hamlet, he has built himself a villa : the kind of villa one would like to run away with. Approaching it by a grassy slope, one is overcome at every step by a sense of the sublimity of its surroundings : the southern precipices of " Il Cervino," ever-present but to-day evanescent behind their shifting drapery of heavenly mist, dominating everything. On the terrace of his villa, facing his " beloved mountain," I found my friend. We already knew each other by correspondence on the only theme—the Alps. Among my mountaineering memories I shall always hold dear that first meeting with one who has done so much to pass on to others the enthusiasms and exhilaration of his own wonderful achievements. His climbing days, he tells me, are over ; but nothing else with him is ' over.' Let those who love the Alpine classics re-read his *Matterhorn*— surely one of the most attractive works in all the literature of climbing. On this first visit I did not linger, my host sketching for me a programme for the afternoon : a visit to the "Lac Bleu" with an invitation to come back early in the evening in time for dinner.

I discovered the Lac Bleu nestling in the woods— its marvellous turquoise-coloured waters reflecting the upper crags and snows of the great chain, with ' Il Cervino ' crowning all in undisputed sovereignty. As I lay upon the turf by the lake, realising that (apart from the mosquitoes) I had reached one of those spots which we are justified in calling an earthly paradise, two or three Italian youths came and sat down near me. I found them to be young people camping in tents in the valley. With my scraps of Italian and their scraps of French we pieced together a pleasant conversation. Presently they were joined by others until I found myself sitting in a group of a dozen of *la jeunesse italienne*, very attractive, very young, almost childlike in their enthusiasms and laughter ; happy, care-free children of Nature. To the spirited vigour of these *gioveni* was added the delicate charm of their girl companions, whose presence completed the poetry of the circle. One of these—whose name proved to be Julia and whose age was vouchsafed as 19—began to sing. It was all very enchanting. Could anything be more so indeed than this company gathered together at such a spot, so obviously in love not only with one another but with their mountain home. Upon request Julia sang " Valencia," whose rousing notes interpenetrated the green sprays of the larch woods and spread through the glorious air. " She has a beautiful voice, has she not ? " quietly remarked one of the youths who acted as our chief interpreter. They invited me to join them in their next day's outing : the long, long tramp by the Théodule to the summit of the Breithorn. I could not accept this invitation, but I was with them in spirit

in the still hours of the night when they began to stir
in their camp by the mountain stream, for they were
to leave at 3 a.m. Happy young people with their
overflowing friendships and childlike unaffected loves,
I hope that they enjoyed the climb !
We parted when evening was coming on, but not
before a group had stood upon the lake shore to be
photographed as a foil to the majestic outline of the
mountains on which the shadows were already falling.
Far up in the fleecy clouds and now and then showing
its crest of snow lighted by the evening sun towered
the Piz Tyndall, which at certain moments might be
taken for the summit of the Matterhorn itself. But
presently the clouds moved on, the sunlight glinted
upon the snowy crest far higher, and once again the
peak of peaks became revealed.

Leaving my *gioveni* to return to their tents, I made
my way by a grassy path along the bank of a small
torrent, to the villa of Guido Rey, whom I met coming down the slope with two visitors : an older and a
younger man. Who could these be, I asked myself ?
I was not long in doubt as to the younger man step-
ping alertly down the path, for I soon recognised the
familiar features of one of Italy's national heroes—
the Duke of the Abruzzi. How favoured I felt when
my host presented me to this great explorer and
"sweet prince." "Are you staying up at the hotel ?"
he asked in his attractive English. " Then I shall no
doubt see you again presently." The older man was
one of the leading members of the Duke's expeditions,
who had been with him " everywhere." Later in the
evening, on returning to the hotel, I met the Duke
again and we spent (for me) a memorable time sitting
on an old-fashioned sofa with refreshments laid out
in front of us. The North Pole, the photography of
Vittorio Sella, the Mount Everest men, the life and
work of Guido Rey : these were some of the subjects
we discussed. His climbing days are perhaps at an
end now : his life is so crowded with various interests
that he does not think he will again climb. A touch of
fever contracted in Africa had brought him here to
the Val Tournanche for a fortnight in its invigorating
air. With his friend he left next morning for the
two-hour walk down the valley to " civilisation." He
was bound for Courmayeur, where he was going to

67

inaugurate a memorial to one of his guides now dead. Everyone at Breuil thought the Duke perfectly charming, and it was not surprising that a group of guests gathered round him to bid him adieu—as he left in the cool of early morning.

Here comes a break in William's account of his time in the Val Tournanche, so comment can be made on the fact that wherever he went or whatever he was doing, he seemed to attract unusual contacts and experiences of great interest, or is it perhaps that others may have similar things come their way, and they pass without any impression worth speaking of? As this next instalment of Alpine excursion says, William always felt the urge to *share* his highlights in life – this was deeply ingrained in his nature:

THERE are some experiences which one would gladly share with others if one could, but which by their very nature must largely remain personal and unshared. I cannot hope to do justice to the absorbing interest of my evening with Guido Rey. In the simple ideals of his summer life at Breuil there seemed to be something Tolstoyan. The first touch was given by a peasant woman peacefully cutting hay on the slope below the villa. Then in the background, lads could be seen playing at bowls. These were young visitors to the valley whom my host had invited into his grounds, to enjoy themselves. A rippling brook flowed merrily down from the woods above : a Tennysonian kind of brook, giving Nature's consecration to a scene of peace and beauty.

The villa (designed by Guido Rey himself) is substantially built of stone and is so arranged that the terrace or ' stoop ' on which he spends some of the happiest of his leisure hours, faces direct on to the Matterhorn. His niece from Turin was acting as hostess, her husband and their little boy completing the charming home circle. Presently under the welcoming glow of the oil lamps we sat down to dinner. The cumulative effect of the long pull up over the Furggenjoch had been telling on me for some hours past and no meal could have been more welcome, more truly enjoyable. But from the cultural standpoint it was an even more memorable event. On such occasions, in the presence of a spirit infused with so catholic a sympathy, it is well to say little and to listen much. But I could not listen only ! Too filled was I with enthusiasm for this meeting with my host and with admiration for the glorious world of the Val Tournanche around me.

Guido Rey presently produced some long Italian cigars shaped like Chinese chopsticks. With the smoke of these rising gently from their glowing ends, we continued our conversation (or communion is perhaps the better word) far into the evening. My host has made a special study of some of our great prose writers and I cannot help thinking that his artistic and literary gifts—Italian as they are in essence—bear something also of the impress of the English mind. Among our Alpine classics I believe that the writings of Leslie Stephen have given him as complete a satisfaction as any. His friend Edmondo de Amicis spoke of him as a man " to whom the motto ' Excelsior ' has not been merely his climbing motto but the guiding principle of his whole life." A fine and testing phrase ! Rey is a lover of his fellow-men—especially of the less privileged in life—and among his varied gifts, his sympathy with the lives around him may well be the greatest, the rarest. He has done much to encourage the scheme of holiday camps in the mountains, for the young people from the cities of North Italy ; and in his summer retirement he is never more pleased than when sharing his enthusiasm for the Val Tournanche with one of these latest-comers to this classic ground of the Alpine pioneers. Looking down on little Breuil from the terrace of his villa he had pointed out to me the chalet which had served as de Saussure's headquarters during the latter's visit in 1789 (?). It is always refreshing and inspiring to tread in the footsteps of pioneers. As the years pass on these footsteps fade and disappear, but here at Breuil this ancient building with its sturdy dark old beams looks safe for many generations to come. May the inhabitants of the hamlet respect it until its last timber fades into final, inevitable dust !

69

Those who propose to visit Breuil should assure themselves of accommodation in advance. Given the sublimity of the surroundings, I was not surprised when the landlord of the hotel told me that every bedroom was engaged. I did not do badly, however, for the bathroom was placed at my disposal for the first two hours of the night and an attic for the remainder ! Up here under the eaves I opened a small window and looked out into the living night. Bright stars were shining over the barrier of peaks, the only sound in the valley was that of running water (the sound as of a distant sea on an ocean beach), whilst lights twinkled here and there in the valley below. And so to sleep ! . .

From a doorway on the terrace of the hotel there emerged into the sunshine a figure whose acquaintance I was soon to make : the Italian guide, Leonardo Carrel—a veritable man of the mountains. The name of Carrel at once recalls the heroic days —for Leonardo's father was the famous Jean-Antoine, the story of whose death on his beloved Cervino, in August, 1890, forms one of the most moving passages in Alpine literature. As to Leonardo—a young man of twenty when his father came to his heroic end, he is now himself the well-tried veteran. With his lined and bronzed features and his great unforgettable moustachios, one feels as one moves steadily behind him that here indeed is a man to count on, a true figure in the great tradition. I engaged him for the return by the Furggenjoch to the Matterhorn, and we left Breuil in the hot sunshine of the afternoon—accompanied by Guido Rey's nephew, Sr. Carnevali, who came up from the villa to enjoy this opportunity of a five-hour tramp in the upper reaches of the valley.

Carrel has a peculiar and well-tried step which continues steadily, unerringly. Scarcely does he utter a word in an hour—just occasionally " A gauche, Monsieur " or " Ne bougez pas, Monsieur ; attention ! " " Deliberate, silent, sure " must be his motto. I have been in the company of many guides, but never have I seen such impressive sure-footedness. And what a background is that silence of his ! What adventures and experiences, licit or illicit, does it conceal ? Only when the sky-line ridge or the ultimate prize has been won does he relax, and taking off the *rücksack*, invite one to inspect and to enjoy its contents. I fancy that Thomas Carlyle would have loved Carrel : the man of action and not of words.

Turning our backs on Breuil, we climbed the great slopes of grass where lonely shepherd boys enjoy the solemn grandeur of the mountains, and rising higher and higher, came at last to the chaos of rocks already described. Thence over screes on to the snowfields, where thunder and dark clouds warned us to hasten our steps. Then rain and mist. It was time for my companion to return to Breuil : so, reluctantly taking leave of him, Carrel and I continued our way to the summit of the pass. By evening the clouds had cleared, and we could look down on the chaste stretches of ice which encase the eastern foot-rocks of the Matterhorn. After a careful descent in the twilight we were soon stand-ing on the rain-washed surface of the Furggen glacier—from which a stiff pull of a thousand feet brought us to the Belvedere—that familiar resting-place for the ascent of the Matterhorn. Here we were joined by the Zermatt guide, Leo Gentinetta.

A pleasant night and sweet dreams and then into a world of glorious sunshine we stepped next morn-ing from the cold passage of the inn, to rope up for the final climb. Circumstances delayed our start until 9 a.m. By this time the rocks were already warm and every ledge and crevice and *arête*, so often negotiated by lantern-light, had the advantage of being visible, comprehensible. Carrel led the way up the rocks and across the snow-filled couloirs. By middle-day we were resting in the Solvay hut (poised in a vertiginous position at 4,000 metres). By 2 p.m. we were standing on the glittering, icy summit, enjoying a panorama sublime beyond all language. Clouds were being wafted across the Val Tournanche 8,000 feet below, and only now and then could we see little Breuil, with the sun-shine falling on it. Under conditions such as we enjoyed, the summit of the Matterhorn is a heavenly spot. Let others describe what it is like in storm.

For half an hour we perched on our cold and narrow ledge, enjoying first of all a little food and then the giant scene. Close at hand the dazzling snow-fields of Monte Rosa and the Lyskamm rose from the abyss. Then silently the invading clouds obscured the great peaks one by one, reminding us that we must not linger.

Reluctantly, we turned to go : downward, downward, first over the steep snow-slopes to the rocks where the fixed ropes afford their welcome aid. Then past the " Shoulder " to the Solvay cabin and down the innumerable gullies and walls of schist and gneiss which lead at last, amid surroundings of unforgettable sublimity, to the comfort of the Belvedere. Here, by 7 p.m., we were enjoying our soup amid the spicy perfumes of the kitchen.

Here ends the second account of achieving the conquest of his beloved Matterhorn, so different in the telling, the latter including as it does the much valued visit to Breuil, and the memorable dinner party, and so on. Perhaps it may not be out of place before embarking on the formidable Traverse of the Matterhorn in a first-class storm, which could have ended in disaster, to touch on one or two anecdotes connected with William Bellows' climbing life.

The Manager of his Printing Works in Gloucester remembers 'After he made his first climb of the Matterhorn, he told me that half-way up, he rested his pocket-watch on the ice, when suddenly it started to move. He was about to grab it, but with great thought on his part he decided not to, because he could have gone with it. I well remember he had a habit of taking his pocket-watch off the chain and placing it on the table, especially when he had an appointment to keep'. This would seem to come under the heading of 'presence of mind' which so often came into play in William's path through life, and, one may add, to the lasting benefit to others as well as himself.

The ever compelling urge to share his pleasures with others was largely satisfied by the countless illustrated lectures he was asked to give, when he could re-live and share with his friends his adventures in the mountains. On one such occasion in 1930, he was invited to give such a lecture to the Royal Photographical Society in Russell Square, London, for he belonged to that Society and had often had his Alpine pictures exhibited. In the audience was a fellow mountaineer, Sir

William Griffiths, one time Governor of the Gold Coast. He wrote the following letter to William's mother, still living at that time, though he had never met her:

> Dear Mrs. Bellows,
>
> I must let you know what a treat we enjoyed last night. Your son gave us a delightful lecture on mountaineering, the pictures were lovely, and his comments were instructive and amusing and always entertaining. But there was one thing which gave some of us a 'jar' – when he told us about the experience he had on the Jungfrau in an avalanche, he naturally made light of it, and those who did not understand laughed much at his recital – but those of us who knew what it meant and what he must have undergone in those few minutes, it hurt. Well, it was an experience and he lived to tell the tale, but it is not a thing to be laughed over.
>
> My daughter, who was with me, was much interested and said that she had learned a lot – I felt I had had a trip to Switzerland, and last night I dreamt that I was in the mountains and an elderly gentleman to whom your son introduced me, a big traveller etc., at the end ejaculated one word 'GOOD' and it *was* good!
>
> Please thank your son for his lecture and believe me,
>
> > Yours sincerely,
> >
> > W. Brandon Griffiths.

Before leaving the mountain scene, the following anecdote adds another dimension of experience, as it were, both to William and his young friend who was the grandson of the afore-mentioned Sir William Griffiths. Holidaying in Zermatt, and staying in the same hotel, John, a 10-year-old, writes Sir W. G.:

> . . . dashed into my room one morning and enquired breathlessly, 'Can I go with Mr. B. over the Theodule Pass? He says he will take me . . .' I did not say 'no' at once, but when I considered the distance I realized it was much too far for him. Luckily his well-concealed disappointment had its reward. Later, it transpired that they were going by train to Rotenboden, and from thence to

Gandegg, where he was sleeping prior to going over to Breuil to see Guido Rey. This would give the youngster a night in an alpine hut. Bursting with pride and excitement, he packed his rucksack. We put in an extra pair of stockings, thick vest, waistcoat and thin shoes – it might have been a North Pole expedition from our careful thought! And in a seventh heaven he went off, beaming ecstatically all over his small brown face, and still enquiring carefully if I would be 'alright, and not too dull or incovenienced', as he quaintly put it!

Next morning my bedroom door opened abruptly at 9.30 and a whirlwind rushed in. 'It was lovely . . . lovely'. He was almost too full of enthusiasm to speak coherently. Evidently he had enjoyed it to the full.

Since then, there were further expeditions for these two down the years – 'John' *did* fulfill his ambition to become a member of the Alpine Club, and over 40 years later writes:

My grandfather was a good judge of people and well aware of the many unusual characteristics William Bellows hid beneath a calm and mild exterior. Determination, quickness of action in emergency, attention to detail and quality, and unhesitating willingness to risk danger for others – qualities I could see for myself in a small way in my young days, whether stopping a nasty slip one day on a snow slope, or being taken round the (printing) works, the excavations, and the Bungalow on the Beacon, or watching him play tennis in Zermatt, and not least meeting at least one of the shattered refugees from Nazi Germany, staying and working at his home.

It has been said that William Bellows 'endures', rather than enjoys general society, but with a circle of chosen and cultured friends he is happy enough, so imagine how delighted he was when one day in 1940, quite out of the blue, a member of the 1926 Everest Expedition phoned to ask if he might call at William's Gloucester home. Although his wife was laid up with a cold at the time, so anxious was he to share the honour of this visit from N. E. Odell, that a rendezvous of short duration took place in the bedroom, generously spared from the all-engrossing interchange of climbing talk. Mr. Odell, 40 years later, remembers William for his warmth of personality, and wishes he had seen more of him.

CHAPTER VIII

Miraculous Survival
traversing the Matterhorn

SO FAR, ONLY CLIMBS under ideal conditions have been recorded here, but there must be few, if any, serious mountaineers who have not tasted the ominous hazards of bad weather, magnified out of all proportion in the heights.

This chapter is therefore concerned with William Bellows' experience of being 'caught' in such conditions, and how they miraculously came out alive.

He describes this climb in August 1927 as follows:

AFTER the usual toilsome climb from Zermatt, I reached the Belvedere (10,820 ft.) and turned in for the night. I do not care much for the Belvedere. The short night, the noise of heavy boots, the nerve tension which refuses food and leads to querulousness, the food itself, the uncertainty as to what tricks the weather is going to play, all these conspire to take the gilt off the gingerbread. But one asset I must not fail to mention, and it cancels out all these defects at a stroke: the splendour and the glory of that unforgettable panorama.

On waking at 1 a.m., I looked out from my narrow bedroom window into the still night. The stars seemed to hang like glow-lamps in the air. The giant obelisk of the Matterhorn was visible to its very summit, where it died away into the night. It seemed to be beckoning me upward. Its *real* message, if I could have read it, was

76

however, 'I think you had better leave me alone to-day.'

At 3 a.m. came knocks on every door, and heavy boots began to move—a suggestion, at any rate, that the great peak might 'go.' I came downstairs and joined the semi-silent group of yawning climbers. Remembering my past experience I avoided the 'coffee,' and indulged in a small omelet. My guides, Leo and Otto Gentinetta of Zermatt, were finishing their breakfast. 'Well,' I suggested, 'it does not look so bad outside, does it?' 'It is fine now,' they replied, 'but we don't much like the look of things. The wind is in the wrong quarter.'

We agreed to start, however, and roped up. As we approached the first rocks (3.25 a.m.), it was evident that the conditions were not normal. The white sugar-loaf appearance, so familiar to us at Zermatt for days past, was on the mountain still. Instead of making straight for the rocky spine, we worked our way well round to the right, and after scrambling up some steep snow, zigzagged back on to the familiar ledges. No lanterns were necessary for the moon had risen in a bank of cloud, and its subdued light was enough for us. From rock to snow, from snow to rock we mounted, steadily upward. Suddenly a brilliant light shone upon our footsteps from behind. The moon had sailed out from its bank of cloud, and was shining on the rock with wonderful brilliancy. The 'Belvedere' was already far below, whilst Monte Rosa and her sisters were peering at us in their moonlit glory through the abyss. Presently there came the light of dawn, often so cheering and full of hope, but to-day uncertain and somewhat sinister. Then the sun rose behind the Rimpfischhorn, all the colours of the spectrum tossed high into the sky, and every peak glorying in the sunrise splendour.

At the Solvay hut (13,124 ft.) I said to myself,
'Now for a "breather" and for one of those pears
in the rucksack ! ' But L. G. had his eye on me.
'We must not linger here,' he said. 'The fine
weather isn't going to last. We had better get on
at once.' I gave L. G. half my pear, and in five
minutes we departed. That was the only halt of
any consequence in thirteen hours. Soon afterwards I noticed that filmy clouds were beginning,
ever so innocently, to girdle the summit of the
mountain.

We climbed the steep rocks immediately above
the hut, and worked our way slowly and cautiously
up that frosted treadmill, the Shoulder. Then we
began to negotiate the fixed ropes, which were in
an icy, most unpleasant condition. Other climbers could be seen above us on the ropes, and one
or two of these, we heard later, had unpleasant
experiences on their way down again to the ' Solvay.' A keen wind was blowing, and it became
colder. All the rock crevices were filled with
matted cakes of frozen snow. My guides asked
me if I thought it were worth while going on, as
the conditions would probably be too bad for the
descent on the Italian side. On a ledge we discussed the possibilities of success or failure, and
decided that, as an hour and a half should see us
on the summit, we would push on for the present
and take counsel again later. Older and wiser men
turn back, no doubt, but one cannot always be
older and wiser. And when one's verdict is
reinforced by the strength and ardour of two first-
class guides, what more can be said than that we
were the victims of a form of mountain madness
not to be understood by dwellers on the plains.

A further pull up the remaining ropes and we
were on the snow. Another fifteen minutes would
bring us to the summit. But the driving clouds

prevented our seeing much until, at 9.40 a.m., the Swiss signal mark (14,781 ft.) suddenly emerged from the gloom only thirty yards above us. We grasped it for a moment, as if once again to touch *terra firma*, and passed along the summit ridge, with its beautiful cornices crowning the cruel, unplumbed precipices and abysses which descend to Italy. We declined the pressing invitation of the wind to visit the Zmutt valley on our way, and stumbling along in the increasingly unwelcome blast, reached the Italian signal-mark, which had evidently been struck by lightning. I wonder if a shorter visit than ours was ever paid to the top of the Matterhorn ? It seemed disrespectful to come and go so quickly. Yet this was no place for a halt ; so different now from the same spot just twelve months ago on that summer day when we sat upon our coiled-up rope in sunlit space and, glorying in the sublime spectacle, 'skimmed off the visible cream of creation.'

We decided to descend a little on the Italian side and finally test the conditions. It is a wonderful moment in this 'traverse' when one begins the downward plunge ; impressive at all times, but now full of mystery and foreboding. With firmer grip and tightened rope, and with an impatient kind of caution, we began the descent. In half an hour any question of a return to the summit had passed from our minds. We had, in fact, by this time burned our boats, and knew that if we were to find safety at all it must be at the Italian hut (12,763 ft.), four or five hours further on. Otto G. led down the rock, his brother bringing up the rear. Then suddenly the crisis came ; in other words, the storm proper in its vilest mood. As we rounded a buttress on the exposed precipice, the wind hurled itself at us in a frenzied icy blast—a triumph of mountain devilry—filling the air with

79

a million particles of driven snow ; not the soft
snowflakes of a Christmas card, but frozen atoms
which bit into our eyes just when every ounce of
vision was needed. Those who live in safety far
below may disbelieve, if they wish, the legend that
these high peaks are inhabited by evil spirits. But
up here in the wild fury of the storm, the mountain
was now obviously alive with them. They were
dancing on every ledge, chasing us down the rocky
walls and jeering at us from every icy shelf. The
streaming, angry gusts followed one another, as
with half-closed eyes we dropped from ledge to
ledge, from slab to slab, setting our teeth and
moving with the utmost speed which could be
reconciled with caution. There were moments
when the wind would seem to be abating. Then
it would come back with a fiercer blast than ever,
when it was safer just to remain anchored as still
as possible on the ticklish rock, which seemed to
dip away into clouds and eternity below us.
Continuing the storm-swept *arête*, it was always
our bad fortune to remain exposed to the blast, for
it was necessary above all to keep to the true line
of descent, much as one would have given for the
shelter of some friendly ridge. We came to the
fixed Italian ropes—the ropes I had so often heard
of and longed to see and handle. I had asked for
ropes, and ropes I was to have ! Here they were
—white and icy. We dropped and dangled down
them at almost incautious speed. Oh, for a fairy
godmother to hand me some new warm gloves !
My own were quickly 'icing up' with the cold, so
I took them off and lined them with a pair of socks.
But this manœuvre having been noted by one of
the malignant spirits, the ropes tore my gloves off
and made things worse than ever.

From time to time a slight thinning of the clouds
would reveal an unsuspected presence, some

gigantic buttress of rock disappearing into the unseen depths, something vast and near to us but soon obliterated, giving us just a passing vision and then cloud again.

The Gentinettas took full advantage of these glimpses. Amid it all, and in spite of the tension of the descent, who would not have been overcome by the sublimity of our surroundings ? Even in this storm and on these cruel crags it seemed, in a sense, good to be here, to be privileged to enjoy at close quarters and, indeed, almost to take part in this superb and never-to-be-forgotten spectacle of the great peak at bay.

The cold, coupled with the short night's rest at the Hörnli, ended by making me feel sleepy. It seemed so tempting just to take a nap and forget it all. But there remained to me enough sense to realise the danger of this state; for here was a far more subtle enemy than the chance of a slip. If I had let things go, and in a quiet moment given up the struggle, I imagine that the end would soon have come. There was no pain at all : just a not unpleasant numbness, a sense of oncoming oblivion. I roused myself and told the guides, and they gave me cognac. I shook myself, concentrated on the details of each step, forced myself to remember our position, compelled myself to wakefulness. From the shelves of sullen rock hung icicles, huge and sinister in their dark lairs. And then there were stalactites of frost, pearly grey in colour and lovely in form, forming curtains and fringes. At one point the wind wedged its way behind an array of this frosted drapery, ripped it off and tore it into bits, hurling them into the air and mixing them with the flying snow. 'Cognac, please, cognac ! ' I cried—and oh ! how grateful were those meagre thimblefuls ! Along and down the slippery ledges we passed, but how insecure it all seemed, even when the rope was passed round knobs of rock for anchorage, and how cold and slight the finger-holds on those exposed and icy corners. The guides kept manfully at their task, hardly speaking. Slipping and dangling down further ropes, Otto G. and I landed on our respective ledges, Leo as 'last man down' performing the hardest task of all by prodigies of balance, encumbered with ice-axe and bulging rucksack. I hated the sight of those ropes, and still more their icy sting, but where should we have been without them? And what of the pioneers who came and went this way before there were such things as ropes? All honour to the men who worked those early miracles of climbing! Then there was the famous ladder. There is an almost vertical descent just above it, and as I came down I could see its three cables lashed over a ledge. It was anchored at the bottom, but was tugging and shaking in the wind, white, sinister, evil-looking. I clambered on to it and dropped from rung to rung. Whether firm rock lay a hundred or a thousand feet below me I could not say, for beneath was cloud. Leo was shouting from above, but I could not hear him in the storm. Half-way down the ladder—and clinging tighter than one does to the poles of an electric battery—I obeyed the signal and turned round its outer edge with my back to the precipice, to drop down the remaining rungs.

Thus piecemeal we came to each famous passage in turn—the Cravate, the Linceul, the Mauvais Pas. The visibility continued as bad as ever, and owing to this we missed our way once or twice and (easy temptation!) got too far down, retracing our steps silently and laboriously upward. Yet how any one in such a storm could find *any* way at all was a marvel to me. And oh! those icy slabs licked by the clouds and dipping one below the next like giant tiles on a giant spire, I cannot forget, and I can hardly forgive, them. Once or twice in weak moments I began to ask myself, 'How is this going to end ? Is it really well with us ? I doubt it very much.' We came presently to something which always tends to make me hesitate—a disappearing snow-slope of ruthless steepness. I prefer the ruthlessness of rock, which, after all, is a form of *terra firma*, even if attenuated ! I had purposely left my ice-axe behind at Zermatt. One could do without it on the rock, but here how welcome it would have been ! Yet this slope must be faced and dealt with. Steadily we advanced across it, the rope anchored to the straining ice-axes, and held tight by L. and O., myself between them, silent and very insignificant, and digging my fingers where possible into the axe-holes in the frozen snow above me. These things teach one perspective and a sense of proportion, for on such a slope the little things of life cease from troubling. You must stand upright and keep a steady head, advancing when told to, and then standing still again as if all were well. A splendid subject for the camera on a fine day, but to-day in this chilling storm, ugh ! . . . And yet who would ever forget the spectacle of that slope of purest white descending, mysteriously descending, and passing out of sight into the gloom below us.

It was now four o'clock in the afternoon, and we were nearing our goal. Still keeping to the *arête*, still dropping, dropping, tormented by the wind, yet taking each step with the utmost caution, we presently beheld our arctic Mecca. Below us on a shelf of rock (we could have jumped through space on to its roof) lay our hut, the Rifugio Luigi di Savoia, half-buried in the drifted snow. A short but unpleasant passage lay between us and it, but our 'bar' was crossed at last, and in thirteen

hours from the 'Belvedere' we forced open the
double door and entered the darkness of the cabin
(12,763 ft.). We remained here for eighteen hours.
The first thing was to get warm. There was a
stove, but no fuel. We held a conference by
candle-light, and decided to chop up and burn the
only chair. The hut rapidly filled with smoke, in
which my guides moved about like Mongols in a
Gobi cabin. The wind raged outside, and became
more frenzied still when it failed to blow our hut
down the precipice. Getting my things off, I
covered myself in rugs, and withdrew in the darkness to the wooden shelf, where I spent twelve
hours sleeping or trying to sleep, and trying to get
warm. The bang-bang of the axe continued at
intervals through the night ; now an arm and now
a leg of the chair was being turned into smoke,
through which our stifling candle glimmered. One
of us tried to open the little window. As the
shutter was pushed back there was a shriek of wind
followed by a smash of glass. So that was that,
and henceforth it was a case of candle only. At
Breuil I reported this damage and the consumed
chair to the leading guide of the Val Tournanche,
and in due course settled the account for their
replacement. Our clothes and rucksacks were hung
round on nails and wires to set up the illusion that
they were drying. The strange low dialogue of my
'Mongol' guides ended every few hours with the
welcome query, 'Meester Bellows—a cup of soup,
a cup of tea ? ' Oh, that soup and that tea, I
wished there had been more of each ! There was
just the difference between them that there is
between nectar and ambrosia. Meanwhile the
storm continued through the night with great
force, making the hut tremble, creak, and drum,
which caused us to feel grateful to the Italian Alpine

Club that they had put such solid workmanship into their 'rifugio.'

At 10 a.m. the next morning, after cleaning up the hut and barring the broken window, we forced the outer door open and braced ourselves for the remainder of the descent. I say 'braced' advisedly, for things still looked very nasty. One would have thought that by this time we had worn down the patience of the storm. But no, the wind at once grasped us by the throat and bade us be gone as we seized the long rope drop and descended the chimney just below the hut. It was difficult work pressing downward under such conditions, when every foothold seemed precarious and when the slightest slip might still be disastrous. But whatever the temptation to shorten the descent, we were compelled to keep to the line of the *arête* in the full 'line of fire' of the wind. The clouds were still around us, but time was telling in our favour, and soon the great precipices began to stand out more and more. We reached the Col du Lion (11,845 ft.), and strode along its lovely curve of corniced snow, whence the plunging view into the abyss of churning gloom on the Tiefenmatten side would have satisfied both Dante and Doré at a single stroke. Circumventing the Tête du Lion (the 'Tête' of which we could not see), we crossed further snow-slopes and steadily worked our way downward over the great rock bastions towards safety. The driven snow now turned to sleet. This was a distinct gain, even if it meant melting icicles and dripping clothing. Presently the clouds opened further, and far below us lay . . . *Italy;* and, most welcome sight of all, little Breuil at peace in the valley, with its tumbling torrents and waterfalls. Then we came to the first flowers— frail little things growing in rock crevices. We halted at the memorial to Jean-Antoine Carrel, at

85

the spot where the old man died, his duty so finely done. Those who visit Breuil should not fail to walk up as far as this point, not only because it was here that one of the greatest of Alpine guides laid down his life, but for the splendid view of the precipices of the 'Italian' Matterhorn on which he strove and conquered.

As we strode on down easier slopes in easier mood, a marmot peered down on us from a rock. We whistled and shouted at it, but it would not move. Why should it, indeed ? As the guides said, ' few hunters come this way, and it knows what it is about.' We hardly deserved it, but this marmot seemed to be sneering at us. Well, so let it be, we said, and passed on. In another hour we were enjoying the delicious reaction which set in as we reached Breuil. It was worth a full measure of toil and discomfort on the heights to feel as we now began to feel. We made for the Italian inn near the torrent which races through the hamlet— a simple hostelry, but just the anchorage we needed for our storm-battered selves. The landlord set before us three large bowls of hot tea, and a stir was made in the inn to work up simple comforts for us. Leo and Otto G., the true heroes of the traverse, must have been glad to set down their bulging rucksacks. ' Il Cervino ' still looked angry in its storm-cap, but from this our quiet sanctuary we could now laugh at it.

Leaving the Gentinetta brothers chatting with Italian colleagues at the inn, I strolled down to visit my friend Guido Rey at his summer villa by the larch-wood, for he was expecting me. He was taking a siesta when I reached his home, so I spent a quiet half-hour sunning myself on the ' stoop ' and enjoying the preliminaries of an all-round drying by the kitchen stove. Oh heat !—delicious heat !—is it not, after life, perhaps the greatest of God's gifts to man ? Presently the door opened and in came my friend and host. ' Ah, mon ami,' said he, 'si j'avais su que vous traversiez le Cervin par ce temps-là, j'aurais passé une *bien* mauvaise nuit ! ' However, here we were, safely anchored in the little port of Breuil, and the sharp memory of our discomforts already melting in the Italian sun. Tea was served on the terrace facing south, the sunlight acting on me as a delicious and all-healing balm. Signor Rey brought out his photographs and explained to me, in detail, the route by which we had come. It was easier to follow it here on his study table than it had been up there *in situ !* Then, while my host rested towards evening, I went for a stroll in the larch woods on the mountain-side, the ground literally over-run with bilberries, juniper and mauve gentians, and the song of water coming up from the valley below.

We who had descended that afternoon from the clouds were fortunate in being able to enter Italy without let or hindrance. For some time past there had been difficulties on the Swiss-Italian frontier, and climbers who had drifted too far down into the Italian valleys had been turned back by Fascisti guards. But thanks to the kindness and foresight of my host, the authorities at Valtournanche, a few miles below Breuil, had been warned of our coming, and had sent particular instructions to the frontier guards not to disturb the ' Englishman with guides ' who was to pass this way ! Nothing could have been more courteous and agreeable than the resulting arrangements made by the Podesta.

I dined and spent the evening with my friend, and together we discussed the Alps from end to end, and Italy, and Life. Then, bidding him farewell,

I returned by lantern light to our inn by the torrent, my mind running on those memorable and truly delightful hours at the villa. Having found my simple whitewashed bedroom, I at once turned in and soon collapsed into the heavy sleep of the mountaineer.

The next morning we toiled up the long slopes to the Furggenjoch, crossed the pass in thick cloud, descended in a thunderstorm to the Schwarzsee, and with long strides disappeared through the rain to Zermatt.

Thus ended our hazardous yet glorious experience of a first-class peak during a first-class storm. Full of gratitude for having come through safely, and of admiration for the exceptional skill and uncomplaining fortitude of my guides, I pass on this story to my friends.

And a fitting contribution indeed to the part of this book which has been devoted to the side of William Bellows which never tired of the glories of snow-capped mountains and the efforts needed to scale them.

CHAPTER IX

Public Life in Gloucester
and Winning Through Opposition

IT IS TIME that attention is turned towards the backbone, as it were, of William Bellows' life – the everyday round of life, the bread and butter part, as well as the responsibilities to the environment, and to Gloucester in particular.

He was born in and spent the whole of his life against that background, and spectacular though his trips abroad may be, it was the utter devotion to his home town and the caring for the welfare of all he contacted in his day to day life that earned for him the loving respect in which he was ever held, and underlines the point already made of the balance he gave to his incomings and his outgoings. This is what makes the story of his life not so much exciting and out of the ordinary, but satisfactory and heart-warming. After his death, a friend wrote to his widow, 'All your life long, your heart will be warmed when you see the look on people's faces at the mention of his name'.

His printing business was of course always there and claiming his full attention, for the firm was founded on a reputation for good quality, and he himself was its best representative, visiting customers all over the country and making them his friends, and, in his own inimitable way, bringing in good business based on trust and confidence.

William was also responsible for, and this too has been indicated in a previous chapter, revising and bringing out further editions of his father's French-English Dictionary. This would necessitate visits, often lengthy, to Paris.

He belonged over the years to many Societies, indicating where his interests lay. These included the Cotteswold Field and Naturalist Club, the National Trust, the Committee for the Preservation of

89

Rural England, the Royal Photographic Society, the Rotary Club, the Royal Society for the Prevention of Cruelty to Animals, and the Gloucester Ratepayers Association, and giving talks and picture-shows wherever he was invited to do so. This can easily be referred to in a large collection of press accounts and handbills in the possession of Gloucester City Library.

William did not spare himself in these directions, but, turning to his civic responsibilities, this is a story of many struggles and heart-searchings. His nature was such that when he was inwardly convinced of the rightness of some project or other, or alternatively of the unwisdom of such, he would pursue what he considered to be his duty unswervingly and conclusively. When he was in office as Alderman of the City, he earned the name of having a 'nuisance value', which really meant he would not be put off his chosen path, no matter what it cost him, and many were the 'brushes' with the Mayor and others over such questions as a measure to enforce the adoption of the Humane Slaughterer in the abattoirs, or the refusal to support a gigantic sum to be used for a grandiose scheme for a new Civic Centre. Invariably the process was a painful one for vested interests had to be exposed. In some cases it took years of determined effort to achieve the desired result.

There was a time when William seemed to make the headlines daily whenever the City Council was in session, for the foregoing reasons, but the public loved him, they had cause to, and the following incident came to light when studying the record of civic matters preserved in the Library. It happened that he defaulted over renewing his driving licence, owing, as he said, to the pressure of public affairs and also that no reminder had been sent. However, the magistrate saw fit to fine him the maximum sum and he protested, not to having been fined, but to the magnitude of the fine which he said was out of proportion to the offence, but there was to be no let-up. Next day, the following letter appeared in the *Gloucester Citizen*:

AN AMAZING FINE – to the Editor of the *Citizen*.
Sir,

A line of protest against the astonishing and amazing fine inflicted on one of your City Aldermen by a brother Alderman for a petty infringement of one of the laws under the Motoring Acts.

The fine is out of all proportion to the offence – one tenth of that would have met the case.

The imposition of such a penalty shows an extraordinary lack of judgement. It seems almost like a public insult to one of your most prominent and useful citizens.

Yours,

'Onlooker', Stroud.

Also:

Sir,

In tonight's *Citizen* I have read 'Onlooker's' protest. I feel truly grateful to him. He voices, I am sure, the feeling of many Gloucester people. I do not belong to the peaceful 'friends' and in no way connected with the highly-respected family of Bellows, yet when I read of this amazing fine, I was simply dumbfounded.

It may be law, but I am certain it does not represent even the average citizen's idea of common justice and mercy – much less those of superior intelligence.

Signed – One of the Many.

But the matter did not rest there, for it transpired that the magistrate had wanted to exact an even higher penalty, but this was pointed out to exceed the legal limit. Such matters are apt to linger on in the public mind, and although it would seem that William was put in the position of scape-goat, one almost feels sorrier for those in authority who reveal characteristics not as noble as they should be.

The final judgment upon William's work through the City Council can be safely placed in the hands of those who 'observed' and could make considered assessment. The following appeared in the press after he had been elected as Alderman, and speaks for itself.

The City Council at its last Meeting before vacation, got through quite a lot of important business. It is fashionable to talk about 'the Council in its wisdom', but for once I must congratulate the Gloucester City Council upon the exceedingly good taste and sound judgement it has shown in electing Mr. William Bellows to the aldermanic vacancy. No name is more honoured throughout the county and there are few who have done more to further the best interests of this grand old city than the new Alderman. I am sure that from every point of view he will be a distinct asset to our administration.

(N.B. W.B. was elected 21 to 5.)

The lasting monument to William Bellows' memory locally was perhaps the bringing about of the purchase of Haresfield Beacon and surrounding acres for the Nation by the National Trust, and as it is a long story in itself, and with many facets, not always at the time fully understood, this story will more suitably occupy a chapter to itself.

William laid down his office as Alderman in July 1938, after 12 years service in that capacity.

Meanwhile, to jump the years, since the following act of public service was his last before his life was taken in 1942, it should be included here with what has already been recounted.

It was during the War, when Gloucester and its surroundings were all too familiar with the noise of testing war vehicles which were made near by, and these passed frequently along the road past Tuffley Lawn and through Whaddon and Brookthorpe up Horsepools Hill. Now at Whaddon was a very beautiful avenue of elms, which had been planted to commemorate the victory of Waterloo – an avenue alongside open spaces used gratefully by the city dwellers, for it was within walking distance of the town centre and a favourite picnic spot therefore.

Having been away from home for a day or two and driving through Whaddon, there was the alarming sight of two of the giant elms felled to the ground. This needed looking into, and immediately William set about an enquiry. What transpired was that previously an Army lorry had driven along that road when a branch had fallen upon it – so in due course, the War Office decreed that the whole avenue should be sacrificed. But this was not good enough for William, who like his father before him, had a deep reverence for beautiful trees. He at once got into touch with the Forestry people in the Forest of Dean, who agreed to send an expert to examine the trees which were still standing but doomed by the authorities. A detailed report resulted advising tree surgery where necessary, and given that, the avenue was good for some 20 more years.

By this time William Bellows had retired from public life, nevertheless he was in a position to work from behind the scenes as it were, especially as the Lady of the Manor of Whaddon, Mrs. Jeune and a friend of his, had gone to him saying 'Mr. Bellows, what shall I do? I have already sold the timber to a contractor'. On investigation this same contractor stood revealed as the Chairman of the C.P.R.E., so no wonder he was far from pleased at the interference!

However, the whole matter had now gone to the Gloucestershire Highways Committee, and at their meeting at the Shire Hall in September 1941, it was reported as follows:

> The Gloucestershire Highways Committee, at their meeting at the Shire Hall today, agreed in principle to the preservation of the elms at Whaddon Green, and appointed representatives to make investigations.

> The General Purposes Sub-Committee reported that they had under consideration the possibility of preserving the avenue belonging to Mrs. Jeune, who, in view of the danger to road users by falling limbs, had ordered the felling of the trees. The Sub-Committee were able to stay the felling of the trees and had obtained the expert advice which showed that, while danger existed, the condition of the trees was not beyond remedy whereby the avenue could be preserved for another 20 years.

> The Sub Committee among other proposals recommended that the question should be referred to the County Planning Committee, with a view to the County obtaining control of the trees, and that representatives of the Committee should be given power to investigate the matter.

> A long discussion followed, Mr. Ellery, remarking that the avenue was one of the nicest in the county, said that the news that the elms must be felled filled many with alarm. He thought the county would be acting well within its powers in preserving anything in its area which made for beauty. In particular, many people were concerned that the tree life of the county should be preserved as far as possible.

> Mr. J. Peter observed that while he was with Mr. Ellery in preserving amenities, at the same time, they should give every consideration to the preservation of human life.

93

Mr. R. G. Hanks said that if they preserved the trees, their life would not exceed 20 years, and the Committee were entitled to know what the cost would be before embarking on a scheme of that sort. Timber was badly needed at the moment, and many owners had had to submit to the national effort. It would be better to let the trees go and plant young ones for the benefit of the future generation.

Mr. E. Machen enquired whether, if the trees were preserved there would be any security against an order to fell by the Government for timber.

Lt.-Col. Godman pointed out that the Timber Control had always been ready to consider representations made by Planning Authorities.

Mr. Wilfrid Nicholls said he would prefer the trees to be trimmed to look tidy for 20 years, but he was not sure it could be done. He advocated the planting of young trees to take the place of what he was sure would be, in 20 years time, ugly old elms.

Capt. J. H. Frye expressed the view that it was inadvisable to preserve the trees temporarily. Long before 20 years had passed the avenue would not be a thing of beauty. He felt very strongly that the best thing to do was to let the present elms go, and replant. He moved an amendment to this effect. Mr. L. L. Potter seconded.

Sir Frederick Cripps, Chairman of the County Council, said the view of experts was that young trees would not grow in the place of old elms, and to flourish they would have to be 100 yards away from the highway at Whaddon.

Capt. Fry disagreed. On being put to the vote his amendment was defeated, and a motion by Mr. Alpass that the Committee agreed in principle to the preservation of the elms and appointed a committee to investigate the position, was carried.

The reason for inflicting this rather dull report of Committee proceedings on the patient reader is to show how hard it must often be to men of wide vision, albeit public-spirited, to suffer the dreary 'dragging of feet' which must all too often go on in local government.

The outcome of all this was that the elms *were* successfully treated, the Lady of the Manor *did* plant a row of chestnuts some feet further in from the edge, and the only real loser in all this affair was the Timber Contractor. Now the chestnuts have grown and all trace of elms have gone, and increasingly few left to tell the sad tale of the Whaddon Elms. Seats which were placed in key positions at each end of this avenue in memory of William Bellows, who worked so hard in the public interest, have long since been destroyed by vandals.

One further instance of local misjudgement which cut William to the quick was when the ancient and beautiful wall on one side of College Court, so close to the Cathedral precincts as well as having historical value for its own sake, was ruthlessly destroyed and gave place to what William described as a 'Dartmoorian wall' (part of the British Home Stores) in a leaflet he printed called *Goths and Vandals*.

But history clearly shows, that to aspire in any degree to public life, the lesson which is most needed is patience, and to learn to suffer fools gladly, if possible.

CHAPTER X

Haresfield Beacon presented to the Nation
– involving Stanley Baldwin

WHAT A FAR-REACHING PART Haresfield Beacon played in William Bellows' life and afterwards. This beautiful spot was near enough (just five miles in the car) to take frequent walks there and so to get away from the daily demands in so many directions. And with him always a faithful companion, at one time 'Boodles' a sealyham of great character who became notorious for his mischievous damage, but fiercely devoted to his master and in later years his place was taken by 'Ian', a canny Scots terrier, a sweeter character certainly, but a dog who definitely knew his own mind!

So Haresfield Beacon was a favourite spot for peaceful relaxation of mind and spirit.

It is a promontory of the Cotswolds, 713 feet above sea level, and stands out between Gloucester and Stroud. It overlooks the great bend of the Severn with the wide waters of the distant estuary, the ranges of Bredon, Malvern, the Forest of Dean and the Welsh hills. On clear evenings can be seen the Brecon Beacons 50 miles away, and sometimes the outline of Exmoor, 75 miles to the south west.

The Beacon and the two spurs to the immediate south of it form a group of wild down and woodland still entirely unspoilt. A Roman camp of the 3rd century occupies the extreme point of the headland, and just above it, at a height of 834 feet on a neighbouring estate, lies the early British Camp known as Broadbarrow Green.

Surely this was a delectable spot and greatly to be treasured for posterity. William certainly coveted a simple little bungalow perched up and overlooking this vast expanse, and in time made this known to the owner who had built it for his invalid wife. However, it soon became evident that the altitude did not suit her, so he offered it to Mr. Bellows in June 1930.

HARESFIELD BEACON
Lord Dickenson handing the deeds to Stanley Baldwin for the National Trust

VIEW FROM HARESFIELD BEACON

Overjoyed at his good fortune and at the same time plans having been on foot to acquire the Beacon and its surroundings for the National Trust – this to circumvent some ominous development schemes – he agreed to forego some of his recently purchased land in order to improve the project. The assumption held sad to say, by a few, that he had engineered the whole scheme for his own personal benefit was quite wrong, and only underlines the essential need in any such situation to know the full facts before passing judgment.

Some months later, in January 1931, when the Haresfield Preservation Committee had successfully completed their appeal for private contributions, the ceremony of handing over the land to the National Trust, represented by one of its officers, Mr. Stanley Baldwin, later Prime Minister, took place amidst evidence of great public interest.

It was a great day for the locality, and given here is William Bellows' own account of it as it happened on 10th January:

> Saturday morning was a very busy one. I cleared up my work as rapidly as possible, had my 'Riley' car polished up and petrol put in, went out and bought a new hat, and motored to the Midland Railway Station to await Stanley Baldwin who was due to arrive from Astley Hall, his home near Stourport, in his own car direct via Worcester, at 11.15. He had already had a telephone message sent to me through his friend J. C. C. Davidson (from Painswick) confirming the arrangement. He arrived in the Station yard almost punctually – smoking his pipe and clad in a very heavy and enviable top-coat. Hardly a soul was present, except Cecil Turner who had come up with me to help me in case of need, and Richard Hall, the photographer. After dismissing his own car, which was taken back to Worcester to await his return in the evening, he came over with me and got into my car; just as he was stepping in Richard Hall asked him if he might have the privilege of taking his photo – to which S.B. consented with a smile. The resulting portrait was an excellent one. A porter at the station noticed him, and came out, followed by several of his colleagues. Just as my car began to move, the porter put his head in at the window and said, 'May I have the honour of shaking hands with you sir? We did not know

you were coming. Nobody told us'. He seemed greatly gratified to be able to shake hands with his 'leader' – who was in very good spirits. I explained to the porter that we must let Mr. B. enjoy his well-earned holiday! The car moved off, and my companion sat smoking his pipe and seemed in very good holiday form – and looked very well – not any older than his actual years, if that. He said 'We have plenty of time – we needn't hurry'. I asked him if he knew Gloucester and he said that in the old days he used to come over sometimes to attend the board meetings of the Wagon Co. He then asked me for any hints about his Haresfield Speech – any points which we wanted him to be sure not to omit. I gave him a brief outline. I drove the car rather slowly and it was well there was no accident as I became quite engrossed in the conversation. He told me a few little anecdotes about literary people he had known and described his taking Arthur Balfour – after a Cabinet meeting in Downing Street – to see the 'Rima' memorial to Hudson in Hyde Park. I will not repeat the comments of the two statesmen on their inspection of the memorial! S.B. said to me 'It was well that I had not already seen this example of Epstein's work *before* I made my unveiling speech'. I said that I was at the unveiling ceremony and that when he, Mr. Baldwin, drew down the sheet I received a shock. He said 'And so did I'. I told him I had subscribed towards the erection of the monument and had offered a further sum for its removal.

He knew Edmund Gosse fairly well and met him from time to time, and much envied me the little journeys I used to take with him in France and elsewhere. He referred to Gosse's wonderful and 'universal' conversation! Approaching Tuffley he noticed a bus coming with the name overhead and said 'Here we are at Tuffley'. I said that I should be so gratified if he would let me halt the car at Tuffley Lawn and take him in to see Mother 'Now over 89 years old, a wonderful woman, and a very strong sup- porter of yourself'. He said he would delighted. On enter- ing the gate his eye caught the roof of T.L. He said 'How splendid – you have a *real* roof over you. What do you call them – slates or stone tiles or what is the correct term?' Instead of turning in at the front door he strolled along the garden path and explored round by the pond and summerhouse. He took his pipe out of his mouth and asked if he could bring it indoors with him. I said 'Certainly, we must not leave your "alter ego" out in the garden'. Finally I led him into the drawing room where Mother received him with great pleasure and satisfaction by the fireside and told him how ardently she hoped he would soon be in power once again. Hannah and Max, (who were with Mother), also greeted him. He looked at Father's portrait in the drawing room – and referred to the French Dictionary which he said he had known since he was a boy, but finds the type now a little small. After a brief chat we returned to the car – the visit to Tuffley Lawn lasting say, six or eight minutes. Stanley Baldwin seemed thoroughly pleased with all he was seeing. He repeated 'We need not hurry'.

Outside the gate a Tuffley woman (Mrs. Langston) standing there came up and said 'Oh Mr. Bellows, what *am* I to do; the Haresfield bus has not arrived – and how *am* I to get up there? I *don't* want to miss the ceremony. I said 'You had better get in the car, if Mr. Baldwin does not mind'. Mr. Baldwin said 'You know that the A.A. are advising motorists not to stop and give a woman a lift', with a twinkle in his eye! I said 'But ah, this is a *Tuffley* woman!' 'Oh well, that is another matter'. It took her five minutes before she realized that this was Stanley Baldwin himself. She finally said 'Is this *really* Mr. Baldwin?' 'Yes, it is *really* Mr. Baldwin, but I can't take off my hat to you for there isn't room!' He raised his hat which soon touched the roof of the car. Filled with excitement and surprise our fair companion relapsed into silence. The car travelled along nicely – I showed him the beautiful old elms at Whaddon, dating perhaps from Waterloo, the historic farm at Brookthorpe and the old home of Sir Francis Darwin. He spoke of Sir Francis Hyett with whom he was to lunch after the ceremony. 'He reminds me a little of Willis Bund' he said, 'Willis Bund was something of an autocrat but we were very fond of the old fellow'.

Nearing the top of Horsepools Hill, the wide view of the Severn Valley spread out in the wintry haze and the great promontory of Haresfield came into view. He took out his watch and said, 'We needn't hurry need we?' Little groups of late arrivals were straggling along the road, bending their steps towards the Beacon. Many evidently failed to recognize S.B. Perhaps they were looking for a grander car! At the top of the hill the first of the seven motor direction boards which I had helped to put at strategic points the day before, came into view. We were now overtaking more frequent groups picking their way along the muddy lane. The 'car park' in Miss Tidswell's field had a large number of cars already parked there. The lane along to my bungalow was filthy with thawing mud. Outside the bungalow gate a large group of people were awaiting S.B.'s arrival. The evening before, all this lane and area was frozen as hard as iron – now it took the form of thin 'buff' cream. I ran Mr. B. right to the door of the bungalow, about 11.50, on the doorstep of which stood Sir Phillip Stott with a broad grin of welcome on his face and wearing a thick yellowish top coat. Inside, through the labours of Kitty, Mrs. Parker and Edna, the bungalow was looking its best – probably as much was got out of its appearance as was humanly possible! With fires lighted and oil stoves burning it seemed most comfortable and the new curtains added to the general finish.

Here, not only Stanley Baldwin but the leaders of the National Trust (John Bailey, Chairman, Sir Harry Stephens, Sir Edgar Bonham-Carter) and the members of the Haresfield Preservation Committee (except Gogarty and Sibley), also Lord Dickenson and Col. Russell Kerr, were all entertained to hot coffee and other light refreshments.

While at the bungalow the assembled company signed my visitors book, and also S.B. signed a small niece's book 'on a pink page'. Introductions took place and in the limited accommodation of the bungalow, the visitors walked to and fro chatting from room to room, all in holiday mood and tense with the excitement of an exceedingly unusual occasion.

I showed S.B. my special map of the West of England seen from the bungalow door – and also the photo of Sir Edmund Gosse and Thomas Hardy which I took at Max Gate in 1927. He laughed and said 'Gosse looks rather dressed up in good style, does he not? He liked to be seen in good clothes, I think'.

After 20 minutes or so of coffee-conviviality in the bungalow, we trooped outside and I got them to stand in a semi-circle in the hollow by the old stump of oak (garden seat) and with Mr. Baldwin in the central position I photographed the party. The weather was still and slightly misty although the trees on the summit of May Hill were just visible. If one could not see the entire expanse of that marvellous landscape one could at any rate imagine it from the beautiful foreground and middle distance.

In little knots we dispersed down through my rough 'garden' and made our way to the central plateau of Shortwood, to the point where a huge trunk of a fallen beech lay prone upon the ground. This was the spot where the dedication ceremony would take place – just where the grassy slopes began to round off towards Haresfield Beacon, and with beautiful views into the valley below.

The public were now making their way across in clusters from various points towards the chosen site, and by the time the ceremony began there must have been 500 present.

It had all along been our intention to hold the ceremony on Haresfield Beacon should the weather permit (as it certainly now did) but two important London 'Talkie Films' Companies had sent down talkie film recording apparatus in huge motor vans and had discovered that these were too large to gain access to the Beacon and that they had not sufficient electric cable to reach out to that spot, so at short notice it was decided to transfer the scene of operations to the site at Shortwood – and the police (under Major R. C. Little) at once herded up the public from the Beacon to this spot. It was not long before the crowd of 500 had gathered round the fallen beech on which stood our Chairman of Haresfield Preservation Committee, Mr. T. C. Macaulay – who would open the proceedings. The representatives of the press – London and Provincial – sat with their note books on limbs of the fallen trunk – cameras were evident on all sides and in the hands of old and young many 'clicks' were audible.

Speeches were delivered in this order:

T. C. Macaulay – opening
Lord Dickinson of Painswick –handing over the deeds
Stanley Baldwin – accepting for the Nation
John Bailey – Chairman of the National Trust
Sir Harry Stephen – member of the N. T. Council
Lt.-Col. Russell-Kerr – vote of thanks
Stanley S. Marling – secretary.

The speeches were as reported in the press. Lord Dickinson read out his excellent address with the help of carefully prepared notes, and then handed over the deeds which had only just been completed in London. Then Stanley Baldwin stuck his umbrella in the soft turf, placed his bowler hat on the handle, and mounted the beech trunk. Without notes he made his admirable speech – so beautifully worded and so delicate in its Cotteswold feeling. As one watched his features one could see the speech being evolved, so to speak – no hitch at any point but the endeavour to light on the exact word traceable in the expression on his lips.

There was a comfortable feeling here – no constraint or restraint among the speakers or audience ; all of us happily met together in our common enthusiasm for the sanctity of these wondrous Cotteswolds. When the gathering broke up there was a delightful feeling of sans-gene. The 'great

gentlemen from London' were mixed up with the inhabitants of Whiteshill, Randwick, Haresfield and surrounding districts. I had already written to the schoolmasters of
the villages encouraging them to get their children to come
up here in their numbers. The response from all the
country round was obvious.

I said to Mr. Baldwin, 'And now we have to plant the
beech'. He said he had forgotten that detail – but he
tramped across the level turf, the large crowd following, to
a point I had carefully picked out the evening before; only
one hundred yards or so inside the white gate and forming
a triangle with two fine beech trees standing on what was
formerly my land, and well suited to act as a protection
from the wind.

I had taken the precaution of buying three little beech
trees (two ordinary and one copper beech) and we selected
the sturdiest of the three – an ordinary beech about 2' 6"
high in a large pot (we now broke it), Mr. Baldwin remark-
ing that we must have 'an ordinary beech'. This particular
one was supplied by Hopwoods of Horton Road. A pit had
already been dug by Artus (of Eastgate) and some fine soil
and manure brought up by G. W. Hogg of Whiteshill,
who was there in his Sunday best. This used to be his land
here. Charles Gere held the tree upright while S.B. wired
away with the spade (bought by me that morning) and
filled in the earth. By evening the tree had been well
staked and fenced against rabbits. This tree planting
ended the proceedings. I can keep my eye on the beech
from the windows of my bungalow as it is well in view –
and it may one day rise up into the sky and interfere with
the superb landscape.

It was now about 1.30 and the company broke up –
crowding up the lane with Mr. Baldwin and the other 'big
men' – and gradually drifting away towards Stroud or
Gloucester or the local villages. The weather had been
very kind to us. We had taken a risk but had won out.
Many miles of country could be seen in the still light of
winter – no wind – no keenness in the air. The grass was

cold from the recent frosts. People crowded round to get a chance to shake hands with S.B. who – as he tramped along in his heavy coat and heavy boots, looking very satisfied and ready to joke with anyone within range, might have been the village squire surrounded by his yokels and menials. The lane from my bungalow onwards was in a shocking condition. Miss Hyett and her sister were to motor Stanley Baldwin back to Painswick House to lunch with their father, Sir Francis Hyett. I drove her along the lane to her car, to avoid the mud, and S.B. took the opportunity to get in also, and my little Riley acted as a ferry boat.

At the fork of the land by World's meadow, they alighted and I bade farewell to Stanley Baldwin who left the impression on my mind of a truly substantial Englishman.

After his visit to Painswick he was motored to Worcester by his friend J. C. C. Davidson, and returned home. I remained behind with my guest Leslie Boyce (M.P. for Gloucester) who had come down specially from London for the event, and after coffee and a talk by the bungalow fireside, I motored him down to catch his train at Stroud. I then returned to Haresfield, and with Artus the handyman, cleared up some of the inevitable mess before returning to Tuffley.

And so much for the launching of the 'career' of the bungalow William Bellows counted himself so fortunate to possess, but it continued to make history and this must be related in the following chapter.

CHAPTER XI

The Haresfield Bungalow

AND WHAT OF THAT BUNGALOW, so unpretentious yet so superbly situated – what had the future in store, under its new ownership?

The first concern of William Bellows was to install a visitors book in which everybody who came was requested to put their signature. So what a testimony this book became, containing hundreds of names of friends, high and low, and little groups of people like the Women's Institutes and the local Toc. H who were regularly offered the loan of this beautiful place for outings, and sometimes for week-ends, using the garden as a camping ground.

The first visitors came in numbers not only to admire the situation, but to bring presents for the further comfort and, may be, elegance of the set up.

Living as William did at Tuffley Lawn, with his Mother and two unmarried sisters, Hannah and Kitty, this was the first home he had had of his own, and all the present-giving and congratulation on his newly won prize, took on something in the nature of a wedding affair, for there was ample scope for his many friends to express themselves in a variety of useful gifts, a list of which has been preserved in the visitors book numbering over 30, and ranging from a Wedgewood tea-set to a hearth brush. The only missing article was a Bride!

Humble though the outward appearance of the bungalow was, the owner could not rest until he had changed the exterior from its original red to a dark green to blend in with surrounding pines, and he had paint made specially in London to match the Cotteswold grey for the roof. In time, the building was covered with a wooden trellis to provide for climbing plants, and soon there were flourishing clematis, embellishing its walls.

By June 1931, at the completion of the first 12 months use of the bungalow for entertainment purposes, it is noted that no less than 336 people had been welcomed there.

There, too, met periodically the Haresfield Preservation Committee of the National Trust. What a boon the place had already become!

A brief description of the interior of this simple little building might not come amiss – it had just four rooms and a little kitchen. Rainwater was conserved in an underground tank near by and pumped up (often with great difficulty!) for domestic use. Primus stoves and an Elsan toilet completed the 'amenities', so in no way could there be any claim to luxury, though in future years it was possible to install a calor gas cooker. There was still no electricity for lighting – just lamps and candles.

The fascination of the place lay in the indescribable beauty and peace of the landscape, and the character of the owner whose one desire was to share his treasure and give pleasure and relaxation to the many.

In June 1932, a group of students carried out an exercise of excavating a barrow about 20 yards from the bungalow, and stayed a week there for this purpose. Alas, they had no success, but during that week were visited by a well-known archaeologist, St. Clair Baddeley of Painswick.

The beech tree planted on the National Trust land by Stanley Baldwin, and visible from the bungalow, was of continual interest to William, who noted that on 15th May, 1933, it had burst into leaf for the very first time, and thereafter noted almost to the day each year it showed the first leaves of the season.

Stone steps were now built to complete a stone terrace commanding the southern panorama.

The bungalow was seldom idle – for in spite of the many visitors (818 were recorded after the first four years), William himself, accompanied by his little dog, made the fullest use of it as a means of peaceful isolation from city activities, and a place where problems could be worked out in blissful solitude.

And what can be said of the visitors themselves? It would be impossible to take but a few. Suffice it to say that there were among their number some of outstanding general interest, namely, the Hungarian composer Kodaly, whose photograph appears in the visitors book, seated at the sitting room table, quietly writing music. He had visited Gloucester to conduct at the Three Choirs Festival, and the Bellows had given him hospitality. An incident during those days comes to mind when on the Sunday, just as he was preparing to leave for the Cathedral for his concert, it became evident that his baton was so wedged in its case, that nothing could budge it without fear of damage. He flatly refused to use any other than his own, so what was to be done? The time was getting short, and the matter took on the nature of a real crisis! Then inspiration came, and William forthwith made urgent appeal to his dentist, for it was Sunday morning; the baton was safely removed without damage by one of a dentist's delicate instruments, and everyone breathed freely again!

To return to the bungalow, another well-known visitor was S. P. Mais of literary fame, also photographed and included in the book. Then later on appears a photo of William sitting in a wicker chair on the terrace and beside him in a similar chair, is a man with a most remarkable head – he is Señor Salvador de Madariaga who had been a visitor at Tuffley Lawn to attend, and to represent, International Museums, at a Convention in Cheltenham. Sitting beside William in this photo one cannot but be struck by the two most remarkable heads, but so different from each other. It would take an expert to expatiate on this fascinating study.

The bungalow had now become a local institution, beloved by the many and for good reason. In 1938 it came into play in connection with William Bellows' late and surprising romance – but an account of this will find its place in a later chapter which must be entirely devoted to that delectable subject!

Before the war came and had such devastating influence on the whole of the Haresfield district, William Bellows had involved himself in the work of rescuing Jewish victims from Nazi Germany, and it followed that of the many he made himself responsible for, he installed two married couples in his bungalow from July 1939 until their permits came through, one couple to join their son in Brazil, the other couple to go to America.

The full story of how this rescue came about, and of all those who were involved, must be left to another part of this book, for it cannot be adequately told here.

In 1940, William wrote the following, in the form of a diary, describing what led up to the final episode in the history of the bungalow. This concludes the contents of the Visitors Book.

June 2nd A glorious day. Grace and David (stepson) and I went up to the bungalow for a picnic day of sunshine (in spite of the war); we were joined later by Hannah and Gwynedd (stepdaughter) from Painswick. A restful and enjoyable time. W.B.

4th The bungalow was taken over today by the Authorities responsible for the new measure of Voluntary Defence. By appointment Grace and I met the Superintendent of Police, Stroud – Maj. Gatherer and Thos. C. Macaulay at the Bungalow this afternoon – while they inspected the premises with a view to making early plans. At the same time by the aid of a large hand-pump, lent kindly by Will Jones, a start was made in emptying the large rainwater tank (1,500 galls.) which is now much overdue for cleaning. Caudle (from Eastgate) was the leading operator of the said pump. W.B.

9th We spent this beautiful weekend at the bungalow. On Sunday morning 40 men arrived, representing the villages of Whiteshill, Ruscombe, Pitchcombe and Edge. This was the first gathering of the new Volunteer Defence Corps. They sat out in the open and were addressed by their leaders, M. Stuart of Blenheim, Randwick and W. L. Paul, Longcourt, Randwick. A very striking and enthusiastic meeting. I took photos of the grouped 'ranks' and hope the results will bring out their ardent faces. I addressed the men before the meeting broke up and stressed the need of a *Bren gun*! They are delighted to have use of the bungalow for their local G.H.Q. W.B.

July 21st Grace, Gwynedd and self with Ian went up and had tea at the bungalow. Three men were working on a new telephone line from Whiteshill to the bungalow. The posts are now erected as far as the Sumsion bungalow.

Aug. 18th We all spent most of the day at the bungalow and used the new telephone (Stroud 340) for the first time! No. 1 call to Tuffley Lawn, No. 2 to Clovers (sisters' home).

25th Grace, Gwynedd, Harold Tuke and I spent the afternoon (Ian in Cheltenham).

Nov. 28th At 9.30 p.m. today (Thursday) German bombs fell in the vicinity of the bungalow. One of them fell just inside the wall of Miss Tidswell's wood, about 10 yards below our iron entrance gates. It blew down a piece of the stone wall at edge of wood, and the blast smashed certain windows of the bungalow, but the damage was chiefly inside the building. Some of the asbestos ceilings and partition walls were smashed, various objects (pictures, etc.) were thrown down and damaged and the floors were strewn with broken glass and sheeting. The telephone was put out of order. Very fortunately the bungalow was empty at the time, otherwise there might have been very serious casualties caused by flying glass and broken fragments of asbestos sheeting. The worst damaged window was the small one on left of entrance door, although at right angles to the line of blast. The Home Guard are very kindly undertaking to clear up the mess. Another, perhaps larger, bomb fell in the wood about 30 yards from the one responsible for bungalow damage, bringing down several larch trees. Worse still an incendiary bomb fell by the doorstep of the Birmingham's cottage – a very serious and most unpleasant happening! Other incendiaries fell in the neighbourhood. W.B.

Dec. 1st Home guard cleaned up the 'mess'. Crowds arrive from Whiteshill to inspect the damage!

1941

Jan. 18th A high official of the Air Ministry (from London) called on us today and *commandeered* the bungalow property as from 20.i.41.

Mar. 6th The Air Ministry write to cancel the above arrangement.

Unhappily or happily (according to how you look at it in retrospect) the story of William Bellows' Bungalow at Haresfield does not end there, though it had to be left in other hands in its sad and pathetic condition; for years passed before the rightful owners were allowed to renew acquaintance and start efforts to reinstate this war casualty.

Meanwhile, other and bigger issues occupied the mind, for William fell sadly ill, underwent an operation in November 1941, and after recovery and later a relapse, laid down his life on 29th March, 1942, so he did not live to take part in the ensuing phase of the history of his beloved rural refuge, so lovingly cherished, so lovingly shared.

Not until the War was over and the R.A.F. had relinquished occupation of the bungalow – (for in spite of dilly-dallying noted in William's diary on March 6th, it *was* commandeered and occupied by men who must have been bored to have left the place in such a parlous state) – was it allowed to visit, let alone take over the property once more.

From a financial point of view it was bad enough, for the amount of damages allowed for bomb damage were meagre indeed, and did little to compensate the full extent of disrepair.

Plans went ahead for the restoration, and hopefully for the improvement, of the bungalow which, as has been shown, did not really do full justice to the situation, for it could be made into an ideal home for someone who wished to dwell in a secluded spot such as this.

These plans, architect designed, were duly presented to the planning authorities. Alas, not only were they refused, but an order came that the bungalow must be pulled down for it had become an 'eyesore' to the environment. The reader will surely agree that the matter could not be left there, for, as has been made as clear as possible, it was in no way at all the fault of the owner that the bungalow had reached its present state, moreover with the long delays in dealing with authorities in its forlorn condition, it became the focus of vandalism and thieving. The police would take no responsibility owing to its isolated position.

What then to do? It must be pointed out that had this happened in William Bellows' lifetime, he would have made short work of all the obstacles put in the way of restoration. His widow had no option but to take the matter to law, and the outcome was that the bungalow was allowed to remain, but with *no* improvements, only restored exactly to its original state.

Here will be quoted press reports of the affair:

The Gloucester Citizen, 4th March, 1948

Haresfield Bungalow Controversy

Inquiry told Owner victim of Circumstances

THE REFUSAL OF THE Gloucester Rural Council as Interim Development authority, to give permission for the reconstruction of a bungalow, known as 'Summer Cottage' at Haresfield near Gloucester, which was slightly damaged by bombs during the War, led to an inquiry being held on Wednesday, into the appeal of the owner of the bungalow, Mrs. Grace Violet Bellows, of 81 Twyford Avenue, London W., against the Council's decision.

The inquiry, which was held at the Shire Hall Gloucester, was conducted by Mr. V. L. Nash, F.R.I.B.A. (Inspector for the Ministry of Town and Country Planning).

Mr. P. C. Lloyd who, with Mr. H. A. Gibson, represented Mrs. Bellows, stated that from his point of view it was to some degree a test case of the liberty of the subject.

Mr. D. G. Rogers (Deputy Clerk of the Gloucestershire County Council) appeared for the R.D.C.

The proposed development of the bungalow included the erection of a garage.

In refusing permission for the reconstruction of the property, the Council's grounds had been – that the proposal would injure the amenities of the approach to the adjoining National Trust Property (Haresfield Beacon); that the site was within the proposed Rural Zones in a locality which was not considered suitable for general development; thirdly that the proposal would be likely to create a precedent for further development which would necessitate excessive expenditure in the provision of public services and would seriously injure the amenities of the locality.

Grounds of Appeal

The grounds of appeal were that the bungalow was in existence before the date when the adjoining property was dedicated as an open space under the regulations of the National Trust, and that, therefore, there had been no interference with the amenities of the approach to the National Trust Property.

The reason why plans were more elaborate than would otherwise have been the case was that the Council suggested that Mrs. Bellows should undertake to restore the building at a greater cost than at first estimated. When she took up this point with the Council she was informed that it was not at their request but at the request of the Ministry of Works, and that they were not in any way responsible for the suggestion.

Property Commandeered

Mrs. Bellows gave evidence that her husband, the late Mr. William Bellows, bought the bungalow in 1930. It stood in 1¾ acres, 820 feet above sea-level. In July 1939, it was occupied by two German refugee couples, who made it their home till May 1940, when they were interned. In November 1940, the bungalow was slightly damaged by bombs.

The property was commandeered by the Air Ministry in January 1941, and when it was de-requisitioned in May 1944, Mrs. Bellows took steps to try and get the bungalow reconditioned.

Mrs. Bellows said her wish now was to see the bungalow put to use and that could only be done by restoring it and making it habitable.

Power to Remove the Bungalow

Presenting the Council's case, Mr. Rogers submitted that the proposal went far beyond any proposal to restore war damage and that the restoration of war damage was, in fact, a comparatively minor part of a quite extensive project.

Mr. E. L. Higgins (Planning Officer for Gloucestershire County Council) said that the Planning Committee in making their decision had in mind that at some later stage, under the 1947 Act, they would have the power to remove the bungalow. They were concerned with the ultimate position.

Mr. G. B. Heywood, an adjoining landowner, who attended the inquiry as an interested party, expressed the opinion that at present, the bungalow was definitely an 'eyesore'.

Mr. T. C. Macaulay, who attended as Chairman of the National Trust Local Management Committee, and also represented the C.P.R.E., said that the general feeling of his committee was that the bungalow was not very offensive and that he did not consider that it was an 'eyesore'.

They wanted it to be clearly understood, however, that they sympathised very greatly with the county planning authorities in all their attempts to restrain unsightly development.

At the conclusion of the inquiry, the Inspector and those who attended, visited the bungalow site.

Saturday, May 15th, 1948

Haresfield Bungalow Appeal Upheld

An appeal by Mrs. Grace Violet Bellows, 81 Twyford Avenue, London W., against the refusal of the Gloucester Rural Council, as interim development authority, to give permission for the reconstruction of a bungalow known as 'Summer Cottage', at Haresfield, near Gloucester, has been allowed by the Minister of Town and Country Planning.

The proposed development of the bungalow, which was slightly damaged by bombs during the War, included the erection of a garage. The building stands on the south side of an unmade road connecting Harescombe Hill with the Cotswold escarpment, at a point where the road is crossed by the 800 ft. contour, from which commanding views of a fine stretch of Cotswold country may be obtained.

In a letter which has been received by Mrs. Bellows' Solicitors (Messrs Madge, Lloyd and Gibson), it is stated that, while the Minister agrees with the Council that by reason of its isolation and lack of public services as well as its close proximity to National Trust property, the land would normally be considered unsuitable for ordinary residential development it could not be maintained that the design or external appearance of the bungalow, as it was proposed to reconstruct it, would seriously injure the amenity of the neighbourhood; nor was the structure required to conform with any provisions relating to a building line.

No Option

The Minister was advised that it would be contrary to the provisions of Article 8 of the General Interim Development Order to refuse permission for the development and he had, therefore, no option but to allow the appeal in relation to the development as a whole.

The Minister's decision follows a local inquiry into the appeal, held at Gloucester on March 3rd by Mr. V. L. Nash, F.R.I.B.A., Inspector of the Ministry of Town and Country Planning.

It seemed right, out of respect to all that this bungalow had stood for over the years, and the service to the local inhabitants, and many others, that the whole of this case should be laid before the reader – dull though proceedings of public inquiries are.

Thus, it can be said, the Bungalow at Haresfield Beacon was saved from an ignominious end, and lives on. It was restored to its original simplicity and gave shelter to a succession of tenants until the owner relinquished it to one who, emerging from the sorrows of a broken life, felt that her peace of mind would be restored if she could pass her days in that place of beauty and peace, away from the clamour of world-life.

So ends the history of William Bellows' treasured haven, but the atmosphere inherited continues to give pleasure and solace – long may it continue to do so!

ALDERMAN WILLIAM BELLOWS

THOMAS HARDY AND SIR EDMUND GOSSE

CHAPTER XII

Friendship with Sir Edmund Gosse*
and a Visit to Thomas Hardy

LITTLE, IF ANYTHING, has been said so far directly bearing on the gift
of Friendship, and that after all, is not only the title of the book, but
expresses in a word that for which William Bellows will be remembered, for it is all-embracing in its manifestation. Friendship for the
many, friendship which could wait, and endure if necessary, but
always carrying the power to enrich relationships of all kinds. There
are many little anecdotes which could be recounted to illustrate this
never-failing fount of sympathy on which he drew so readily for the
benefit of others.

These anecdotes will no doubt find a place in their natural context,
but it will surely be of interest to some readers to give a more intimate
account of one particular friendship which was recorded by William
himself and published in a little booklet as a Memoir to his beloved
friend and mentor, Sir Edmund Gosse, Literary Critic and Writer of
repute, and which he dedicated to his widow, Lady Gosse.

This is what William writes:

I REMEMBER so well my first sight of Edmund
Gosse. It was at a meeting of the Anglo-French
Society in London, during the War : a meeting
at which he had taken the chair. I can see him still,
as he came away from the gathering and passed,
alert and erect, into the street. He did not know
that an admirer was watching him from the doorstep as he disappeared into the traffic of the Strand :
an admirer who felt in some peculiar way that in the

*Sir Edmund Gosse, C.B., LEGION OF HONOUR. Librarian House of Lords; Assistant
Librarian British Museum; Writer, Poet, Literary Critic to the *Sunday Times*. Hon.
Degrees Göthenburg, Sorbonne, Strasburg.

whole circle of our literary life there was no one he would rather set eyes on than Edmund Gosse. Soon after this I was introduced to him by his friend Henry Davray, at the close of a luncheon given by the Alsace-Lorraine Society to a French patriot *de passage*. On this occasion also he had taken the chair and I still remember his introductory address and the effect of it on his audience of French and English guests. It was my good fortune to hear him speak in public on several subsequent occasions, both in England and in France, in English and in French. His was the rhetoric of culture ; the phrasing was delightful. One could feel that almost up to the moment of final utterance he was still seeking the *mot juste*—the exact form of scintillating, grave-gay language which would and did so faithfully express his mind. And would that one could convey that intonation, that delicate uplifting of his rich voice which his friends and admirers still remember as a delight. Once, when I was sitting with him by his fireside at Hanover Terrace, he took down Shelley's 'Ode to a Skylark' and read it aloud to me ; and I recall how the very modulation of his voice seemed to re-create the beauty of those matchless lines and to endow them with new song. And how when he came to the words :

> With thy clear keen joyance
>   Languor cannot be :
> Shadow of annoyance
>   Never came near thee :
> Thou lovest ; but ne'er knew love's
>   sad satiety

his voice gently fell and lingered over the lines as if here, indeed, were one of the inmost perfections of poetic feeling.

Following the foregoing reminiscence, William explains that he was at the time working for the Government department over war-

time propoganda and describes the nature of his contacts with Sir
Edmund Gosse in that connection.

> . . . My conversations with
> Gosse quickly showed me how fully he appreciated
> and understood the French point of view in the
> War. He gave me some valuable advice and at
> one time I wondered why his prestige in the
> literary circles of France was not more fully ex-
> ploited than it was ; but those days at the Ministry
> were days when we finally got quite used to
> wondering at things ! In 1916 he had been invited
> by the French Government to visit the Western
> front in the company of his friend, Maurice Barrès.
> He often spoke to me of this visit and of his ex-
> periences in the front-line trenches near Rheims :
> how, for instance, he was anxious to climb up and
> 'look over' until pulled down again by his coat-
> tails by Barrès ! Twelve months later I was myself
> in Rheims—the cathedral scarred by ghastly shell
> wounds, its high altar piled ten feet deep with fallen
> masonry, and the priceless stained glass scattered
> by gun-fire. Gosse cross-examined me closely as
> to the condition of the city as I saw it, and
> it was indeed tragic to note what greatly in-
> creased devastation had come about in the interval.

And now it could continue to blossom, this absorbing friendship,
so mutually advantageous, away from the shadow of war and its
demands, ever deepening in its quality and its rewards.

> It soon became my privilege to meet him more
> frequently. Something was drawing us steadily
> closer. Externally one might say that a common
> interest in France was the cause, but friendship
> may go deeper than that in its origins—quietly
> preparing the ground when we little suspect it. I
> like to think that there are inevitable affinities, and
> friendships which work out 'ineluctably.' Would
> I come up and have tea with him at his home in

Hanover Terrace ? Just a simple cup of tea. I
remember so well the thrill of that first visit to
No. 17. On the first floor was the library and
study. The family life, the fireside life, was carried
on in the front portion of this apartment, with its
fine windows overlooking the soothing greenery of
Regent's Park. In the background was the quiet
study and the writing desk and the loaded book-
shelves. Here in this little corner, one felt, *dwelt*
Literature. If a friend arrived—how many must
remember the experience with delight—there
would be a slight movement in this inner sanctuary,
the closing of a book, the laying down of a pen,
and Edmund Gosse would come forward with extended welcoming hands, and lead one to a waiting
chair—his head slightly thrown back—the strong
earnestness of his face melted down into a delightful smile of welcome. And then would begin that
brilliant talk which was so integral a part of the
man himself, so personal and intimate in its quality,
so unlimited and catholic in its range.

Books and books ! Could any man, could even
he with all his disciplined, methodical and most
practical outlook on the day's work keep pace with
the ever-rising tide of volumes which invaded every
space and corner of his study ? He used to show
me the latest arrivals, still awaiting their turn under
the paper-knife. He was not easily deceived, but
was quick to discover the qualities and defects of
each examined volume. The ore was soon melted
down and I fear he was often, yes often, disappointed ! A favourite word of his was 'slight.'

'Yes—I find this *very slight* : the author is wasting
his time,' and so on. Another favourite was the
word ' ardour.' It was interesting to note how
certain words would thus slip through into
privileged positions. With remarkable ease he would
'run' two or three books at a time by way of

favourite reading. He was particularly fond of
French. He would sometimes ask me what I
thought of a book which we both knew. It was
pleasing thus to be asked my opinion. But I felt
at my ease in expressing my views in such matters
for one of his most attractive and helpful gifts was
his interest in the outlook of younger men. His
was a mind which reached out towards younger
minds and in so doing kept itself for ever also
young. He would sit back and listen by the
fireside, where I can still see him ; and then
would come the simple phrase, 'I am glad you
think so' ; or that other verdict from which there
was no appeal, 'Well, I am afraid I do not agree
with you there—no, I cannot agree with you.' He
had not the gift (indeed who has ?) of suffering
fools gladly ! Like the Rock of Gibraltar he could
bristle with many guns when the case called for it
and I have met with more than one victim of an
unpleasant encounter with Edmund Gosse. They
would go about licking their wounds, muttering
vengeance, and belittling his life-work ; but such
wounds as Gosse himself did not heal were doubtless healed, in due course, by time.

The reader need not feel insulted at a reminder that Sir Edmund
Gosse's most notable writing was most probably the book *Father and
Son*, for although in the last decades it may have been a familiar work,
yet alas, the capacity for reading good literature has undergone considerable change, owing of course to modern methods of communication, such as television. It is easier to acquire knowledge as doled out
from the screen, and so it is only the few who still pursue the delights
of reading and enjoying good English!

He often spoke to me of ' Father and Son.' It
had taken him twelve months to write. I asked
him why he did not produce a sequel to it—the
later years ; I was even bold enough to urge him to
do so, but there was a stop in his mind and I could

never get him to consider the idea. As I came to know him better and to note with increasing admiration his loyalty to his art, I could better understand that stop. 'Father and Son' is a complete literary entity, a perfectly rounded-off chapter of experience ; and Edmund Gosse was too wise a man not, in this particular, to leave well (one might say perfection) alone. His father, could he have lived to see the sequel, would surely not have been entirely disappointed. There were qualities in Edmund Gosse which must have had their origin in those early and so difficult days. For instance, his courage and his love of truth. Others can speak with due authority of the quality of his literary criticism ; but it must have depended largely for its value on that fearlessness of his which did not even spare his friends. 'Father and Son' is a work of genius—of his particular and most indefinable form of genius. He told me with the modest pride which his friends remember, that he thought it possessed something of the 'quality of permanence.' It would indeed be difficult to find a more perfectly finished example of faithful biography : 'a masterpiece,' as Harold Nicolson describes it, 'in which, by consummate power of selection, the author has been able to combine the maximum of scientific interest with the maximum of literary form'. He was gratified when a French edition (humorously known as 'Père et Gosse') was produced. Unfortunately the delicate humour of the original was somewhat lost in the translation, as perhaps all French attempts to render *our* humour must in some way ultimately fail.

As this friendship between William Bellows and Sir Edmund Gosse continued to blossom and world conditions improve, the next phase, and one of the most rewarding it seems, took the form of trips away and abroad which enabled them to enjoy their mutual interests, and it is not difficult to imagine how deeply William appreciated this development.

After the War, when the tension of life became more relaxed and travel easier, I began to enjoy an ever closer contact with him. He frequently invited me to share a spring holiday with him and his wife. In this way we explored together many of the loveliest regions in the South of England and paid three visits to France. Edmund Gosse loved France. His French was rather that of the Academy. I was to do the shopping, he said, because mine was a 'more useful kind of French'! But in this he was too modest. Sometimes he was called upon to address a French audience. He would take infinite pains beforehand. When all was ready he would sit down in some quiet corner and read the draft aloud as if already on the platform. The address which he delivered to an audience of two thousand of the *fine fleur* of Alsace-Lorraine at Strasbourg University, in 1921, was a case in point. I have in my possession the MS. of it—written out in that peculiarly transparent writing of his—so personal to him. It brings back memories of our visit to the de Pange family at Saverne in the Vosges. We spent a week with them in the autumn-tinted forest. The whole country was locked hard in frost—and after a day of exploration we would come home and spend unforgettable hours of 'causerie' in the beautiful book-laden and well-warmed salon of our friends. The night before our visit to Strasbourg, where Gosse was to be honoured by the University, he rehearsed his address by reading it aloud to us. I can see him still, standing under a lamp at a reading-desk in the middle of the drawing-room, and declaiming his message in true French style! He asked for corrections as he went along and the few required were supplied in a tentative, deferential way, by his host and hostess, and even by their little boy Maurice who, full of spirit and with a mischievous little grin on his face, would intervene with : 'Oh, but Monsieur Gosse—we *never* hear that word pronounced like that ! *We* say it like *this* !' As a result of this and other spade-work, the address proved a great success and moved the audience— already tuned up to fever pitch by the 'Marseillaise'—in a way which none of those who were present are likely to forget.

I cannot conceive a greater treat than those wanderings in his company among places—interesting in themselves—which burst into a second blossoming at the touch of his scholarship and understanding. At times he was as happy and light-hearted as a school-boy ; especially if before starting on our journey he had put himself on the right side of his ever-increasing and exacting correspondence and the last letters had been sent upon their journey. A secret of his youthfulness, which continued with him till the last days of his life, was his wonderful combination of memory and of imagination. He could re-live in a remarkable manner the feelings of his earlier years. This made him a companion not only for men and women of his own maturity—but for younger people whose defects he was less apt (and, I think, less anxious) to take note of.

There should be pauses in recounting these memorable holiday experiences which these two friends enjoyed, for they covered quite a few years. William was closely committed to his own Printing Business, and Sir Edmund Gosse equally in demand as a Literary Critic. So perhaps it could be mentioned here that Sir Edmund and Lady Gosse had a son and two daughters, and they were all friends of William's, and remained so. It could have been otherwise, for Philip, the son, was a contemporary of William's and might well have resented the close intellectual friendship enjoyed with his father. The whole family were warm in their attitude towards William, and one can only say this was a tribute to them all, for how often in similar circumstances is it otherwise! In speaking of trips near home, William says:

It is difficult to say which of the southern counties in which we spent our holidays pleased him most. I like to think, and I naturally think, that he was never happier than amid the loveliness of our own unrivalled Cotteswolds! We went over one day to the valley of the Coln. I doubt whether the countryside could have looked more perfect than it did on that brilliant May morning when we entered the village of Withington in my little 'Wolseley.' On every branch a singing bird : the sky rich in wonderful, slowly drifting clouds : the village at peace—and the foliage of the trees almost tropical in the brilliance of its vivid emerald. We halted at the Mill Inn. I thought we could get a nice lunch, here, of glittering Cotteswold trout. Was not the Coln just across the road, winding its way in utter peacefulness through the meadows? No, they could do nothing in the sense I had hoped for : no fish, no hot lunch, nothing but bread and cheese. Yes—we would have that. Edmund Gosse sat on the low wall outside the door while I planned our menu. Bread and cheese and good appetites. In this fine air and in this glorious sunshine what better could we wish than the simplest fare. No sound upon the road except the footsteps of a passing peasant or of a lingering child. Just peace and the slowly drifting clouds. Across the road was a little garden—a miniature lawn whose edge was lapped by the gently moving, most innocent and dreamy Coln. Here my friend sat smoking, resting, thinking, talking. 'We must not expect *too* much of life ; so many lives are spoilt through expecting from life more than life can give.' 'But *can* we expect too much from life,' I asked : ' has it any limits ? Isn't it better to expect too much, to expect everything, and then to rescue *what one can?*' I suggested. But he seemed to think otherwise and with a smile went on with his cigar.

At short notice his talk would become full of delightful *espièglerie* and roguishness. At another inn which we patronized, the landlady was more than a landlady—she was an idealist. She explained to us that she loved the idea of entertaining guests ; that with her it was not simply a case of making a profit out of them. Which caused Gosse to draw me quietly aside, saying, 'Watch the bill ! If I mistake not, we shall find on it this item : To money not being the only thing, *one and sixpence.*'

Max Gate! There must be many who realise the significance of these words and to whom they are related. If not, the continuation of William Bellows' narrative will soon dispel any possible ignorance or forgetfulness. This episode stands out as one of the facets of the literary treasure-house which resulted from the friendship between William and Edmund Gosse, so it is given in full here as it came fresh from William's pen.

29th June 1927 at Max Gate:

ON coming down to breakfast one morning, Sir Edmund Gosse said to me : " William, I have some news for you that will please you : we are invited to go over to tea with the Hardys at Max Gate on Wednesday." From these brief words I quickly realized that ' Wednesday,' already ear-marked for the eclipse of the sun, was likely to be one of the days of my life. . .

The eclipse, with its broad trail of thrills and disappointments, had come and gone, and after a quiet morning recovering from our orgy of early rising, we prepared for our run to Dorchester. Very unfortunately at the last moment Lady Gosse, fatigued no doubt by our previous wanderings through Purbeck villages, did not feel able to make the journey. We therefore made up a party of two only—Sir Edmund Gosse and myself.

The run of twenty-seven miles from Swanage to Dorchester, through Wareham the unavoidable, and Wool the evanescent (I am told it is a village), is a beautiful one. The sun came out and shone on the Wessex countryside, lighting up the blue colouring of the distant moorland, and the foreground of pine, bracken and elder blossom. As the massive clumps of fir-trees dissolved to right and left, fresh vistas of glorious landscape opened before us. Approaching Dorchester I asked my companion how we were to reach " Max Gate "—was it a difficult spot to find, must we go through the town ? " Yes, I think so—I think we thread our way right through the streets—but I am no good at topography—had you not better ask someone ! " By this time we were in " Casterbridge " itself. This little town " possessing " Thomas Hardy, I felt that it would matter little to whom one applied for directions. They would all know ! An old man at a street corner was appealed to. " Max Gate—why you are coming right away from it." " Is it on the Wareham Road ? " I asked : " we have just come from Wareham !" " Yes, half a mile back on the left. You will see the name marked up. There is a cottage further on, but don't go so far as that."

A few minutes later we came in sight of the high brick wall which conceals the house from the main road : the very wall which I had previously seen, and in my ardour, passed. Turning in at the open gate we wheeled along the modest gravel drive among obscuring bushes, to the front door. Here was " Max Gate " : a not-so-old brick house of uncertain size, actually designed by Thomas Hardy himself. The thrill

which had been on me from the first mention
of our visit was now coming to its climax. As
he rang the front-door bell, Sir E. G. turned to
me and said : " My Wife and I were the *first*
visitors who ever stayed here. That was in the
autumn of 1888—thirty-nine years ago." The
door opened and in the inner lobby we were
charmingly welcomed by Mrs Hardy who had
heard our footsteps. A moment later her husband appeared and led us into the drawing room.
And so this was Thomas Hardy—this great little
man with the so familiar features, the melting
little eyes, the lined face and silvery hair and
moustache, standing so erect and speaking with
the clear well-pitched voice of younger years.
When I, the so fortunate one, had been introduced, we sat down or rather settled down to tea
at a large round table drawn into one corner of the
room : a table laden with all good things. Of these
I must not forget to mention the raspberries. Did
better ever grow than these ? " Do you remember " asked Sir E. G. "what Bishop Butler said
of the strawberry ? He said that 'God might
have created a better fruit than the strawberry
but He never did.' Yet He *did*, for He created
the raspberry ! I do not think anything excels
the raspberry at its best." Which led T. H. to
say : " I can never make up my mind which I
prefer of the two. When I am eating a good
strawberry I think nothing can equal it and when
I am eating a good raspberry I think *the same !*"
Sir E. G. " What an admirable and philosophic
spirit. And so wise !" The table at which we were
sitting—was it of dark oak— seemed almost too
large for our little company of four, and I found
myself travelling along my share of its periphery
—to and fro—between Mrs Hardy and her
husband. I could, in fact, have occupied two

chairs in my efforts to catch and enjoy the whole of the conversation.

Two days earlier we had motored over from Swanage to Bere Regis to explore the old church and to see the tombs of the D'Urbervilles. Imagine our surprise to find the latter so desecrated that not a single brass or inscription remained upon the battered stonework. Thomas Hardy was appealed to by Sir E. G. to throw light on this melancholy state of things. This was the work of vandals, he told us, and the metal-work had been stolen. Some sixty years ago a churchwarden had descended into the vault and there had found the coffins still preserved and on one of them a piece of velvet. " What was the velvet for ? " I asked. " Oh, in those earlier days they always used to cover the coffins with black or coloured cloth nailed down with shining brass nails." Then he added " I don't think *I* should care to be buried in a vault." " No " — I suggested — " in damp weather one would soon catch cold down there." From the tombs of the D'Urbervilles the conversation led on to Westminster Abbey, in which T.H. had once seen a grave being dug through the floor right down into solid earth. Taking my courage in both hands I confessed that in the whole of my life I had never once been into Westminster Abbey, adding what Anthony Hope had once said with a smile : " Don't go : don't *on any account* go there. If you do, you will destroy a record which must certainly be unique !" Meanwhile tea was proceeding with a charming informality. How glad one felt that no standardized guests had come upon the scene to ruin everything ! In the liveliest mood (in perfect keeping with that of his friend) Sir E. G. had now settled down to story-telling. He began with one of Lord Kitchener. At a house in Somerset at which he (E. G.) and the great soldier were fellow-guests, Lord Kitchener suddenly exclaimed : " And who *is* this Thomas Hardy you are always talking about ? " which made a stir among the ladies. How could he ask such a question, they said ? Sir E. G. quickly put the matter right and " vindicated our profession " by replying : " Thomas Hardy is a man who belongs to the same ' Order of Merit ' that *you* do, Lord Kitchener ! " On hearing the story, T. H. gave a modest little chuckle and settled down for some more fun.

Nothing could have been more attractive and vivacious than his conversation ; there was no evidence of fatigue, the well-sustained voice showed no signs of failure even at the end of our visit of an hour and a half, and the melting little eyes twinkled all the time. There was a sprightliness not only in what he said but in what he did. I had been speaking to him of the foreign translations of his books. He excused himself for a moment and veritably *skipped* upstairs, coming down with a bundle of paper-covered foreign volumes under his arm. One of these entitled " Tess d'Urberville " had been translated by Mademoiselle Rolland, a sister of Romain R. The Hardys spoke enthusiastically of her English letters : written in such beautiful English that T. H. had never seen them excelled. Sir E. G. here remarked that as a young man he had received letters from Turgenieff, of which the same might be said. " They were written in *perfect* English . . . . I have them still at home." Further books were produced, including an Italian edition of " Tess," bearing the title " Una Donna Pura." T. H. had had some difficulty with regard to translations appearing abroad. He had allowed the translator in this case to carry out the work and to benefit by the resulting profits. " And it was quite a good arrangement for her." Then he went on " It is quite easy to *write* books : the difficulty begins with the business arrangements one has to make afterwards. That is the awkward part of it all. Writing itself is *easy !* "

True to his faculty for recording events and people, William had his camera, and before the visit, had put it in the hands of Sir Edmund Gosse to take the right opportunity of suggesting that a photograph might be taken. So before leaving on this momentous visit the request was put to Thomas Hardy who readily agreed, and they went into the garden, which William describes:

. . . The sun, recovering from the eclipse, had been struggling through the clouds and finally emerged during our visit, to shine in the most kindly mood on shrubs and grass. I had expected to see a tenderly laid-out affair— " the garden that I love " of the true artist. Apart, however, from a very snug little inner lawn adorned with Canterbury bells and a central urn of earthenware, the " jardin d'agré- ment," as the French would call it, seemed limited to trees and formal bushes. At the back of the house Mrs Hardy took me to see the fine stretch of kitchen and fruit garden on to which her husband's study window looks. As we looked up at the window through the trees, I asked her if he were still writing. "Yes—he is *still* writing !" she said.

Fate has cast upon Mrs Hardy the delicate duty of defending her husband from the importunate. It is not known which country provides the largest proportion of these but the United States is strongly suspected. Only last night, she told us, two unknown ladies from California had announced themselves on the doorstep at 8 p.m. Mrs Hardy has a very efficient ' aide-de-camp ' in the parlour-maid, who explained that her master was not visible and that no questions could on any account be passed in. This did not quench them : they still wanted the maid to answer a ' questionnaire ' about her master's personality, and only left on hearing that even this was not permitted.

My two ' subjects ', so amenable to photographic discipline, stood on the front door-step with their hats in their hands. A little grey puss ran out, the friend of the family, and was seized as it whisked round the corner, and brought into the picture. From the porch Thomas Hardy led the way to the urn which formed a suitable ' base ' for a further photograph. I was astonished to see the alertness of his step. This did not look like 88 years ! As we stood upon the lawn E. G. turned to me and said : "William —do you see that tree ? just look up at it ! " Towering into the sky I perceived a pine-tree. " Would you believe it " he said " I once laid my Inverness cloak upon the top of it when we were playing croquet here. Yes . . . . my Inverness cloak. The tree was only a yard or two high then " . . . . I asked " T. H." what was the origin of the name " Max Gate." He laughed and in his ardent little voice said that Mack was the name of an old man who lived up the road and that "when I told my friends that I was building my new home up near Mack's gate, the name stuck to it ! " He went on to say that the ground on which we stood was rich in Roman remains and showed me a bowl of black earthenware which he had himself ' excavated.' " I could find *plenty* of interesting things here if I only went on digging but *what* dirty work it is ! " He urged us not to miss seeing the

museum and the Roman remains in Dorchester.
Mrs Hardy, appearing just then on the lawn,
explained that they were preparing for the visit,
in the coming week, of a travelling company of
players who were going to act a Greek tragedy
for her husband's benefit " on this very grass."
Would the weather be fine ? For it would be such
a disappointment if everyone were driven indoors
by rain. Apparently almost the entire house
would be handed over to the players for their
comfort and convenience : and every passage
would be blocked by their *impedimenta*. It was
going to be a great event—this breaking in on
the perfect calm of Max Gate.

By this time we realized that our visit had
lasted for a good hour and a half and we looked
at each other. It was time to go. Hard as it
was for me to think of leaving, it must have been
much more so for Sir Edmund Gosse whose
friendship with T. H. is of fifty-two years'
standing. As he said to me later, on our way
home, "In the normal course of things neither
he nor I can be here much longer." Yet how
satisfying had been our visit : not a minute lost
and so perfect an atmosphere of geniality and
charm. Mrs Hardy opened a visitors' book and
we signed our names. " My husband used to
write in this when sketching out the plots of his
novels. He tore out the early pages and gave me
the rest of it and we use it now for our visitors'
signatures." " Which road are you returning
by ? " Thomas Hardy enquired. " We think of
going back by Bere Regis for a change." "Then
you must turn to the right and follow the garden wall and then keep round and round to the
right and cross the old bridge. Such an interesting old bridge ! You must look out for it."
He stood on the doorstep with Mrs Hardy as we

turned in the drive and I can see them there still—waving their adieux in response to ours— as we disappeared along the gravel.

We stopped in the open country near Bere Regis, and from the main road enjoyed the landscape which stretches away towards Wareham. It was lighted up by the evening sun and all was still upon ' Egdon Heath.' My companion said : " William, you will remember that visit in the days to come." " I shall indeed," said I.

The most fruitful parts of the friendship between William and Sir Edmund one would say, were those times they spent in France together, and especially that trip which proved to be so near to the end. William writes of these times:

I have said how much my friend loved France. It was difficult to name a French province which he did not know. I crossed the Channel with him three times, each of which he felt would be 'the last.' He called me his *bâton de vieillesse*, I was to let him lean on me in all matters, if I did not *carry* him to Paris he would never go at all : as if he were not himself the most alert and entertaining of all travelling companions. In Paris he would entertain me with the most enlivening memories of his earlier days there. How John Morley had once sent him over to write up the Salon for the 'Fortnightly,' how his friend Hamo Thornycroft had borne him company : how during ten days on end they had lunched on *sole au vin blanc*—a marvellous dish which had become a sacred institution at La Pérouse. Should *we* go to La Pérouse and ask for *sole au vin blanc* and see what would happen ? So we went and asked for it without turning a hair and were served with the same, the self-same dish (no, *not* the same !) forty years later, in the same old-fashioned little room with the low ceiling, looking out over the misty river. But *the* restaurant for us was a discovery we made near the Odéon. We were bowed into a seat near the window, where we found ourselves raised a little above the somewhat whimsical guests who sat around us. There is only one Quartier Latin and although these were no longer the heroes and heroines of Murger's day, they were quite 'somewhat whimsical' enough to call forth our sly glances and suppressed smiles. I think the fact that this was the Quartier Latin gave an added relish to the admirably cooked food and an added zest to our appetite. The landlord intimated with pride that he sometimes entertained Senators here! After dinner Gosse, in this favouring atmosphere, turned back to vivid memories of his literary friends in France. There was an unforgettable and effervescing playfulness in his comments on these men. He knew the strength and the weaknesses of Mallarmé, of Verlaine, of Loti, of Anatole France, from personal contact and observation, and he made their weaknesses appear even more attractive than their strength. As he spoke, one could almost see them, one by one, through the window, working their way down the quiet street.

So full and vital is William's account of the very last trip to France which he shared with Sir Edmund Gosse, that it will be presented in a chapter to itself, and should certainly take its honoured place under the title of 'Friendship'.

Friendship, when it proceeds from a true inner quality can take so many different forms, and to illustrate this, a little story that came to William Bellows' widow long after, may find its fitting place here.

On one of his many visits to Switzerland with friends, he became conscious that all was not well with the girl who waited on them at table in their hotel. He said nothing, but stayed back in order to have a quiet word with her. It transpired that she had had bad news of her mother, but was obliged to carry on with her job in the hotel as if all was well. He showed his naturally warm and understanding sympathy, and next day, according to plan, left with his friends for their next stopping place. Later, those friends returned to England, but

William made some excuse that he wished to go on elsewhere on his own. Instead, he retraced his way in order to have further contact with the sad waitress and see what he could do to help.

He took her address and promised to keep in touch, which he did, adding her name to his already vast correspondence. In subsequent visits to Switzerland he tried to contact her, as she invariably took up the same sort of job in the tourist season. His encouragement to her, and advice in her trouble was something she never forgot, and years later she made it her business to meet William's widow to tell her the full story!

Another, very different, act of friendliness was connected with an elderly Quaker friend who, among other interests, was no mean collector of Japanese treasures – prints, metal work and crockery. William for some time had been in the habit of buying first one piece and then another of this large collection, not because he was particularly interested in such articles, but because he knew that his friend, an old man now, needed the money. When he passed some years later, and all his collection that was still left, was sent to be sold at Christie's, William went to the sale and bought up nearly the whole lot just because he could not bear to think that so many treasures beloved by his friend should pass into strange hands. He would rather acquire them himself, and *give* them to his friends where they would be truly loved.

CHAPTER XIII

The Last Visit to France
with Sir Edmund Gosse

WILLIAM BELLOWS LEFT this full record of his last trip to France with Sir Edmund Gosse:

I now come to the last days we spent together in France—the final days, alas, of Edmund Gosse's active life. We were in Paris together at the end of April, 1928, just a fortnight before his death. I doubt whether (in spite of his obviously impaired health at that time) he had for years enjoyed a greater peace of mind, a greater restfulness of spirit, than on this little holiday. How should we spend our time ? We would spend it in visiting and studying points of Revolutionary and Napoleonic interest. We would let modern Paris recede as in a dissolving view and its place be taken by that city of other days—days of tragic memory—which even demolition will never entirely efface from the minds of men. I had been reading 'Le Jardin de Picpus' by Lenotre. We would go and visit this garden in the east end of the city. Gosse borrowed the volume from me and sat down to read it in his bedroom at our hotel : I believe it was the last book which he ever read. Far from the tramp of tourists' feet and surrounded by a high wall, the Jardin de Picpus only faintly catches the distant murmur of the traffic in the streets. When the guillotine had sufficiently operated on the Place de la Révolution it was removed to the Place du Trône, and Picpus was chosen as its cemetery. A breach (traces of which may still be seen) was made in the high wall, and a huge trench dug in the quiet garden : a trench twenty feet deep. The low-wheeled, red-painted *tombereaux* came here direct from the guillotine with their gruesome loads of corpses which were thrown into this common grave. And here they still lie—André Chénier among them. But of all the tragedies which ended here in this melancholy spot, perhaps the most cruel and poignant was the execution of the Vicomtesse de Noailles (the mother of three little children) who died upon the scaffold in the Place du Trône, with her mother and grandmother, on the evening of July 22nd, 1794. Beneath this turf, under the quiet cypress trees, their mangled remains still lie, with those of 1303 other victims of the scaffold. One of my never-fading memories of Edmund Gosse is that of seeing him as he gazed over the rusty railing on to this sinister and still most tragic spot, in the drizzle of the grey morning : overcome by the living sense of sorrowful emotion which one cannot here escape from. We came away with a feeling of oppression as if we had been looking into the still open grave of one hundred and thirty years ago.

Although this would seem a morbid way of spending a holiday, who knows what these two friends, linked together by a common absorption with France, may not have shared in some past life and their possible need to slough off some shadowed memory?

On the following day we went to happier scenes ; we went to Fontainebleau. We reminded ourselves that by making the journey from Paris and back and taking a fifty-mile motor run in the forest, all in a single day, we were doing more than even Napoleon could ever flatter himself on doing. And I very much doubt whether the great 'little corporal' ever saw his Forest under more glorious conditions than we did. Of course we first visited the Château. We rested like lizards in the hot sun beside the famous steps from which Napoleon bade farewell to his Old Guard. Presently a door opened and a member of the 'new guard' emerged to conduct us through the state apartments. We saw the abdication table, the 'bees' upon the curtains, the famous ceilings, the sleepy courtyards, the porcelain and the tapestries—everything, in fact, of this slice from the history of France. When we stepped out into the sunlight once again we found a waiting motor-car whose chauffeur offered to drive us through the forest to Barbizon for lunch. He told us that he would see to everything : he knew every path and glade and vista and would bring us finally to the very restaurant he knew we needed ! My friend sat back as we rolled along at a pleasant speed through the paradise of trees. The young beech leaves gave a note of the very tenderest green to the scene which opened before us, mile after mile. And here and there, as at Franchard, we came out into the open, to enjoy a far-away panorama of forest country ending in some rich and many-coloured plain extending to the horizon. A day of happy dreaming, with an occasional con-tact with the things of this earth, as at Barbizon. Barbizon, we know, is not what it was—is there any place on earth that is *what it was*—Barbizon, alas, has become an artists' Mecca ! Its early inno-cence has departed, and the line of waiting petrol-pumps in the village street showed us that only by coming here at this early season had we escaped the tidal wave of *tourisme* which the later spring would surely bring.

We lunched in the open air in an inn courtyard. The birds came near us on the sunlit gravel and Edmund Gosse fed them with crumbs. 'Show places' upset him, but we could not leave without

a brief visit to the home of his old friend, Robert
Louis Stevenson, across the street. He never spoke
of 'R.L.S.' without affection and I think the letters
he had received from him through a long number of
years were perhaps his most prized possessions.
Now the sight of a motor-car and the stir of some
passing visitors disturbed him, so we strolled on to
the studio of J. F. Millet—a quaint spot which did
not detain us long, for G. had heard *the sound of
footsteps* on the gravel ! So we were off once more
and with the aid of our obliging chauffeur, we
plunged again into the forest. From time to time
we would leave the car and take a short cut through
the trees. Gosse's spirit seemed to respond so entirely to these surroundings, yet I could not but
note that the shadow of ill-health was not receding.
We had to halt more frequently while he rested on
some fallen tree or lichen-covered rock, and took
breath. But a little rest sufficed and his old spirits
would return. He possessed a wonderful gift of
capping the most casual remarks with lines of verse
and here in the forest he kept breaking into this
playful habit. And often he would improvise lines
of his own if no other poet would come to his
rescue ! Anecdote would follow anecdote and at
some good 'point' he would look up expectantly,
watching the final effect with an encouraging and
irresistible smile. In all my contacts with him I
do not remember his telling me the same story
twice.

It is surely not an uncommon experience that events stand out in
great detail looking back upon them, when followed by an unexpected
crisis like a death or similar shock. William's memory of every detail
of this very special holiday must, one thinks, carry such an explana-
tion. Certainly it was a fitting testimony that he should write such a
detailed memoir of his friend:

Paris, in spite of its satisfying beauty and perfect
outward harmonies, is a city of paradoxes. We woke

up one morning to find Labour Day in full swing,
or shall we say, in full stagnation. Anything more
melancholy than this 'manifestation of the soli-
darity of labour' could not be conceived. The
entire city was thrown out of joint, with the net
result that an enormous quantity of time was
wasted—probably thousands of years by 'linear'
measurement—and untold wages sacrificed. The
only persons who seemed to enjoy the event were
the writers and readers of proclamations to the
people. These adorned the blank walls of side
streets and attracted groups of fiery 'comrades'
and others who would read the flaming headlines
and stroll away with a look of quiet cynicism.
Edmund Gosse implored me to remain indoors
and not to show myself in the streets. He was sure
that I should be picked off by a 'comrade,' as he
put it, while brandishing my kodak from some
barricade ! Later on we plucked up courage and
ventured abroad : but instead of the streets running
with the blood of capitalists and social leeches we
found them running with rain. It was indeed a
dismal affair, this proletarian call to arms, this
manifestation of the sovereignty of the people's
will (for want of a more grandiloquent phrase !)

During our stay in Paris we kept closely to ourselves. Gosse had come here for restful relaxation
and we made no effort to see any of our friends.
On a previous occasion he had been lunched and
dined and conferenced and entertained—and it
was gratifying to note how deeply he was respected,
how entirely he was appreciated, in the highest
circles of French literature. He held a place apart ;
one might describe him as an honorary member
of the French Academy. I am certain that to many
of the Immortals all English men of letters were
personified and resumed in him. He could speak
on literature in Paris with the same authority as

he spoke in London. And here we were in the city of French enlightenment with all this talent, all this scholarship hidden completely under a bushel. But supposing we met with a friend upon the pavement ? Well, he would take the risk. And so he came and went on this last journey of all and with one exception he was to meet no one. The exception was André Gide. He came over to our hotel and had tea with us, two days before our return to London. 'Do tell me what he is like' I asked, just before the bell rang. But no telling could exactly enlighten me as to this very particular and intriguing personality. We had an attractive tea set out in our double bedroom in readiness for him. The door opened and in came our guest, looking (to me) like a 'moine défroqué' —an emancipated rugged little man with a black cloak thrown over his shoulder, and bubbling over with enthusiasm once again to meet ' mon cher maître.' Not a young man any longer, André Gide, but young enough to sit at Edmund Gosse's feet as he listened to his flow of criticism over the tea table. I poured out for them and listened to it all with both ears. Among other matters Gide explained to us his views on politics, French politics with their multitudinous complexities : he would occupy the most dangerous position of all, absolute neutrality, like sitting on a knife edge ! Yes, it is the *middle* position which needs real courage, he maintained. He was radiantly happy to meet his friend, and his face lighted up with an intellectual and literary glow, as Gosse gave him the benefit of his views on his (our guest's) own work. ' And may I not add,' said Gosse in his most attractive and ingratiating manner—the conversation was in English with little bursts of French —' that you often get tired of your characters before you have quite disposed of them ; indeed, that you even get tired *of yourself*. Is it not so ? '

Yes—Gide could not disagree, and he was grateful for this candour. It helped to steel his own courage. How much he had been tried ! Yes, he had his enemies—but then one could not expect anything else when one is out to speak the truth. This ' thé intime,' which lasted an hour, was something rare and refreshing. Gide went away from it with his black cloak once again tossed over his shoulder, out into the evening air of springtime in the streets, feeling that this indeed had been a wonderful hour, an unforgettable experience of intimate and tonic contact with a master mind. I had never heard my companion speak more brilliantly than during this hour. He turned to me when Gide had gone—and said, 'Now William, *do* tell me what you think of him. Did you enjoy it all ? ' But I found it difficult to sum up in words my sense of satisfaction.

And now I come to our last day in France. We would give ourselves a special treat and make a further trip into the country. At first we thought of Chantilly—but Edmund Gosse was anxious to spare himself undue fatigue. His physical condition was not improving and yet he felt that he could still do much. So we began by lunching *au frais* in the Bois de Boulogne, where society people sat about in easy chairs and the birds sang around us in the sunshine. Then taking a taxi-cab which mounted upwards through scores of francs, we made our way to La Malmaison. Who does not know this delightful retreat—who would ever visit Paris without spending a few quiet hours in this ' haunt of ancient (historic) peace.' We walked up the broad gravel *allée* to the entrance, and wandered silently from room to room—examining the priceless contents of the glass cases in which Napoleon and Josephine are brought to life again.

Presently I missed my companion. I found him

resting on a solitary seat on the polished parquetry. After suggesting to me with sly humour 'that one manuscript is as good as another and that having seen one *we had seen them all' (!)*, he proposed that we should go out into the gardens ; the very gardens in which Napoleon had often paced up and down with that knitted brow of his, and which in his usual manner he had turned into a Place of Destiny. We found a shaded seat in a quiet corner and here for something like two hours we sat and talked. One could hear distant voices in the château courtyard and the far-off murmur of suburban Paris, but otherwise we had the world to ourselves. In spite of his occasional discomfort and fatigue, Edmund Gosse was in the brightest spirits. I could not realize that these were already the closing hours of his active life. On this our last afternoon together in France there could be no fore-taste of what was soon to follow. For he was in his best intellectual form, in that entirely contented mood which he so often enjoyed in French surroundings. One has to breathe the atmosphere of France to understand and appreciate what it means. It is a transforming influence—a strangely subtle, spiritual and cultural something which only France can bestow. Paris may reveal this ' something ' but she has no monopoly of it. My friend's sensibility (another favourite word of his) responded to it very intimately and it was not surprising that he was so whole-heartedly contented to be here.

In reading this intimate description, one can feel how deep is the contentment experienced in a real inner relationship such as these two enjoyed, and why William felt the necessity to try and put it down on paper – always needing to share the good things of life with others:

Removing his hat and wiping his spectacles, he began to tell me of incidents from his past life. He especially seemed to emphasize how favoured he had been at many of the turning-points of his career. 'Where others have had to toil and wait, things have often *come* to me. The Librarianship of the House of Lords was a case of this. The post became vacant and it was offered to me. It *came* to me, in fact, and it was just the work I needed.' One of the things which had 'come' to him was the greatly prized friendship of Lord Haldane. He never tired of speaking of Lord Haldane with pride and admiration. He would say to me, 'They do not realize what a great man he is.' There was a weekly exchange of letters between them : 'My dear G' and 'My dear H' passed to and fro with the regularity of clock-work.

Even on a care-free holiday like this he would turn again and again to the all-absorbing and ever-fresh subject of literature, which for him meant life. He gave me a summary of his views on criticism. He found it difficult to place some of the younger writers of the present day, sympathize with them as he might. His view was that as in landscape painting so in criticism one needed a point of observation, with foreground and distance blended in their due proportion. As he put it, it was impossible to bring into the picture objects that were 'too close up to the easel.' Some of these young men were too close up to the easel, for him. And yet I doubt whether any writer of our time preserved a more helpful and sympathetic contact with the younger minds than he did.

This 'landmark' of a holiday was now ended, and preparations made for departure from the country with which they both enjoyed such marked affinity:

On the following morning (May 4th) we were up early to catch our train to England. Edmund Gosse had the gift of doing things NOW. If he had to write a letter, he, unlike some of us, would sit down and write it ; and if a train had to be caught he at once planned the catching of it so effectively that one simply *could not* lose it ! My own method of cutting things rather fine did not appeal to him ; he complained that it produced in him a sense of distress, in fact the most intense mental discomfort !

On reaching London I accompanied him to Hanover Terrace before continuing my journey. Paris had been good but here was home at last and this was better ! His enthusiasm as he began to fill in some of the details of 'our week' for the benefit of the family circle was as delightful and unbounded as a schoolboy's. But under Lady Gosse's protecting care he was persuaded to sit down and rest. Yes, rest he really *must !* The brief minutes were flying but there was still time for a little talk. It had all been so wonderful. 'And what about a little French wine to finish up with' he suggested.

He came out on to the doorstep as I left him to catch my train. He would not have it that it was *he* who had made that holiday. His last words, as he waved farewell, were words of gratitude. I did not see my friend again. On the following day he went into a nursing home. Even there he would courageously take up his pen and keep his friends informed from day to day. Little notes would come from him, written in that luminous and so familiar hand of his, but now revealing an unfamiliar tremor. A minor operation had been performed, a more serious one was to follow. Too ill now to see anyone but members of his family, he was facing the ordeal with quiet fortitude. 'You will think of me in this hour with sympathy and hope. There seems good reason to believe that I shall survive the shock. In any case I am perfectly calm, and able to enjoy the love which has accompanied me through such long years and surrounds me still.' These were his last words to me. He died on the evening of May 16, 1928.

———

These words of George Eliot would seem to convey the very essence of the Friendship between William Bellows and Sir Edmund Gosse, so rich in mutual benefit:—

Friendship is the inexpressible comfort of feeling safe with a person, having neither to weigh thought nor measure words.

CHAPTER XIV

Visit to Mercury Mines
and to Schloss Luegg

IT MAY BE SOMEWHAT IRKSOME to many readers to peruse a chapter dealing with a subject which holds for them little or no interest, and possibly total ignorance – nevertheless the following account which William Bellows wrote of his adventure into Mercury Mines is included here for, if for no other reason, it serves to underline the fact that he was a man who was able and eager to throw himself into a variety of experiences, savouring each venture with a relish calculated to rejuvenate his spirit and send him back to his 'round of common tasks' in Gloucester with yet another ring of experience to add to life.

Here then is an account of a holiday adventure on the Continent where his quest after the unusual invariably paid good dividends:

THE limestone caves and disappearing rivers of the Mendips always bring back to my mind a visit which I once paid to another stretch of limestone country of caverns and disappearing rivers, which has now passed, so to speak, into European history. I refer to the region of the Carso, near Trieste—that strange table-land rendered for ever famous by the desperate struggles between the Italians and the Austrians which it witnessed during the War. Bare and uninviting as the district itself appears, the approach to it from the northward through the Julian Alps is inexpressibly beautiful. I doubt indeed whether there is any scenery in Europe more perfect than that of the upper Valley of the Izonzo, with its soft blue mountain slopes, its most delicate foliage, and running water which seems to come from Paradise. It is at Gorizia that one leaves this most lovely of valleys to climb on to and cross the sterile Carso. The dry-stone walling we know so well on our own Cotteswolds is now visible everywhere—threading its way in and out of the limestone wilderness. Against the clear sky stand out the isolated villages with their *campanili* rising with mirage-like effect into the blue air. In the glare of the summer sun upon this table-land and without shelter or hope of shade the sufferings of the combatant armies must have been terrible. The surface of the Carso is pock-marked with strange basin-shaped indentations known as *dolini*, in the bottoms of which the only cultivation here possible is carried on. Looking down into these little basins one sees vines and other plants delicately nurtured and trained along the scanty soil. Approaching the south-western edge of the plateau a view of another world is suddenly disclosed. The Adriatic—a thousand feet below—dotted with the tiny sails of fishing boats ! On the evening of my arrival the moon was shining on the water, while the lights of Trieste far below sparkled for miles along the lower slopes of the hills, with the blue sea fading away to the southward in the moonlit summer haze.

At Trieste one feels the spell of Venice across the water : calling you westward, westward, only six hours away across the sea. But in travelling one has to sacrifice and prune off many a bud— if one is to grow the perfect flower of a successful journey. As for myself, 'lone-wandering but not lost,' I turned eastward across the southern Carso —to visit the famous caverns at Adelsberg* and the Mercury Mines of Idria.

* Now Postumia.

Would that time permitted me to speak at length of the caverns of Adelsberg. With their many miles of underground river, their glorious massed stalactites and stalagmites of endless shape and beauty—fish without eyes—and dark, still waters mirroring the gorgeous colouring of the incrustations, they are in themselves sufficient reward to repay the journey from England. At one point the roof of the cavern rises 150 feet above the floor, forming a vast hall from which one passes through a narrow passage into a wonderland of translucent stalagmites—one of which rises sixty feet into the air. It is impossible to describe the mysterious beauty of the scene—and one returns at last to daylight—dazed and overcome with a sense of awe and placing this incrusted paradise upon the list which we each make for ourselves of the Seven Wonders of the World.

After further wandering in this unforgettable world of limestone, I turned northwards into Carniola and finally reached the village of Loitsch from which my final objective, the mercury mines of Idria, are distant twenty-one miles.

Loitsch, as I saw it, was a dismal place indeed : rain was pouring down on its forlorn cottages and farm buildings, and the roads were deep in mud. Yet I can well imagine that with its picturesque surroundings and most interesting studies of native village life, it would in fine weather make a charming centre for the traveller.

My doubts as to how I should cover the twenty-one miles between the railway station and Idria were soon set at rest, for in the village I discovered a motor-diligence about to make the journey. One is impressed by the admirable arrangements made in this part of Europe for communicating with remote country districts : well-equipped motor cars threading their way through the tiny hamlets and bringing a whisper of the outer world almost daily to the doors of the peasantry. Through quaint villages our journey lay, with here and there a halt at some wayside inn. This is the country of the Slovenes, Catholics for the most part, speaking a Slavic language as remote from the Italian I had just been hearing in Trieste as Russian is from French. During a brief stay in Finland I once mastered four words of Finnish : during this journey in Carniola I think I only heard five words which were in any sense familiar : the Russian-sounding numerals *adin, dwa, tree, chetireh, piatch,* as the mail-bags were counted out one by one and put upon the roof of our diligence. After four hours of splashing and bumping on the muddy road in well-wooded country, with occasional halts at quaint inns frequented by as quaint a peasantry, we entered the beautiful and deep rocky gorge of the Idrizza, and in a mile or two came in sight of Idria itself : a snug little place rising prettily on the slopes of the surrounding mountains, with the mercury mines dominating the scene.

To introduce the subject of Mercury, William gives this interesting note regarding its discovery:

In the days when Columbus was busy navigating the Western Ocean, it is said that a peasant, looking one day into the trough of a drinking fountain in the village street of Idria, discovered something lying at the bottom of the water : something he had never seen or heard of before. This was in reality a small accumulation of mercury which had come down with the stream. I think they might have erected a statue to the poor man, for this discovery led to the foundation of a great industry which has yielded many millions of pounds' worth of the metal and was still employing

1,300 men after the lapse of four centuries, when I visited the mines.

The story goes that the peasant collected the mercury in a bottle, took it to a town some miles away and called upon a silversmith who, having closely questioned him as to its origin, paid him a few shillings for his ' fluid ' and then quietly went to Idria and bought up land for himself and his friends.

I was told in the village that if I wished to visit the mines I must apply to the director at an old castle on the hillside. To this peaceful place I accordingly repaired and found myself in the courtyard of a beautiful old residence dating from 1527, now used as the *Direktion* of the mines. Here were to be seen some huge and rare specimens of cinnabar or red sulphide of mercury, containing, I was told, up to 75% of pure metal ; rock specimens far too heavy for anyone to carry away. After waiting in a quiet office the ' Herr Direktor ' came in and asked me if I would like to see the mines. He seemed interested in this visit of an Englishman, and told me that I was the first of my kind to come there during his tenure of office. He then handed me a signed pass, and said that if I would go back to a certain point in the village a miner would meet me and take me underground.

William here interrupts the narrative to make some helpful observations regarding Mercury, its history and its uses. Apparently there is no mention of mercury or quicksilver in the Old Testament – but the metal was known to the Greeks and is referred to in Greek writings of the 3rd century B.C., but long before this it was used medicinally both in India and China. The Arabs, who inherited the medical lore of the Greeks, used mercury as an ointment for the cure of skin trouble. With regard to the Almaden mines in Spain – they had been in existence since the Roman times, and 10,000 lbs of cinnabar were sent from them annually to Rome in the time of Pliny.

Mercury is the *heaviest natural liquid known* and it alone posses-
ses as a metal the property of melting at ordinary temperatures. If,
however, the temperature of the metal be reduced to —39°C., it
solidifies into a tin-white mass which can be beaten with a hammer
or cut with a knife. At normal temperatures the specific gravity of
mercury is 13, that of gold being 19, and platinum 21. But a curi-
ous phenomenon takes place if its temperature be reduced until the
above-mentioned solidification sets in; owing to the drawing
together of the molecules during solidification, the special gravity
of the metal rises by over six points, when it surpasses that of gold.

Mercury is found in the metallic state in small globules, and in
very small quantities only, in various parts of the world, but it is
chiefly obtained from its red sulphide and in this form it is mined
in Idria. Pure cinnabar contains 86% of the metal, but the ore
yields a much smaller percentage than this, falling at times as low
as 1%. At Almaden in Spain it averages 5% to 7% and increases in
richness with the depth of the mine. Returning to the visit to Idria:

The extraction of the metal is carried on in
furnaces in which the broken-up pieces of cinnabar
are exposed to oxidizing flames which volatilize
the mercury : the resulting greyish-blue-coloured
fumes being carried off through stoneware tubes
to cooling and condensing chambers in which the
metal is ultimately deposited. It is then filtered
through canvas and packed in iron jars with
screwed stoppers, each jar holding 76 lbs. of the
metal. From the mines of Idria these jars are
conveyed to the nearest railway, whence they are
distributed all over the world. The commercial
mercury which we see in our thermometers is
almost chemically pure. It can be finally refined
by forcing it through chamois leather or allowing
it to run through a very fine hole : or chemically
by allowing it to fall in a fine stream through
sulphuric acid. Prior to the War, the world production of mercury was about 4,000 tons per
annum, of which Idria contributed from 600 to
700 tons, the principal other sources of supply

being Spain, Italy, California, Texas and Russia. At one time the Idria mines and those of Almaden supplied the entire world. Quite recently a rich find of mercury has been made in Japan—but it is not likely that it will be exported, as Japan herself will absorb the total output.

What becomes of the 4,000 tons of mercury which I have mentioned as being at any rate the annual pre-war world supply ? It is very largely used in the manufacture of medicinal preparations, in thermometers, barometers and scientific apparatus, in dentistry, in the manufacture of electric lamps, in that of vermilion and explosive compounds and in the amalgamation of gold and silver ores, but for this latter purpose it is now used much less than was formerly the case. Speaking of amalgamation, it is interesting to refer for a moment to this extraordinary property of the metal. According to Professor Gowland, 'it combines or amalgamates readily with gold, silver, tin, zinc, lead, and bismuth : but it will *not* unite with platinum, iron, aluminium, nickel, and certain other metals. All amalgams are white and are solid, pasty or liquid according to the less or greater proportion of mercury they contain. When the amalgams of gold, silver and the heavy metals are heated to the boiling-point of mercury (360°C.), the latter vaporizes off and leaves the other metals behind. It is on this property that the extraction of gold and silver from their ores depends.' Absolutely pure mercury does not adhere to a surface unless that surface consists of a metal soluble in mercury. Thus if you place the least quantity on a sheet of paper, it forms a neatly rounded-off globule and if such globule be subdivided it breaks up into a number of equally beautifully formed globules, which, when brought together, will quickly coalesce. Should there be a small proportion of lead or zinc present in the metal, the latter will then 'tail off' and leave a filmy streak behind it.

These details may well be of interest and in any case, of instructive value, as they make this venture into the mercury mines more than just another experience. William goes on:

To return to the mines ! I did as I was instructed and met my guide at the appointed spot. He carried an acetylene lamp and a hammer. The ancient portal on the hillside through which we passed into the lower regions bore the date '1500' carved on the stonework overhead. As we passed inwards into the mountain side it was difficult to avoid stumbling or striking one's head against the rocky roof of the low, ever-descending, darksome passage. After walking downhill perhaps for a quarter of a mile we reached in a dark recess, not a pumping station or anything of that kind, but a fully-equipped and well-arranged underground chapel, a place of devotion for these worthy miners on their way to work. Candles were burning on the altar. Soon we began to descend ladders and the already noticeable heat became greater, whilst frequent openings would indicate passages to right and left leading into other parts of the mine. Twelve hundred men are employed in the underground workings, and another hundred are busy on the surface at the furnaces, which I subsequently visited, in which the metal is extracted from the native cinnabar.

Although no large or open space was anywhere visible, every passage and gallery being exceedingly confined, the whole inner mass of the mountain must by this time be simply honeycombed by the multitudinous passages and galleries. Large beams of wood support the rocky roof above your head, and the mercury ore is dug out in horizontal layers of a yard in depth. At one point my guide stopped, hammer in hand, and searched along the reddish rock which lined the sides of the passage. Then, throwing the rays of our lamp on to the living ore, he struck off some fragments which he put into my hand ; and there in the bright light shone out the oozing beads of native quicksilver. Since that moment when the glint of the liquid mercury gave such a fascination to my strange surroundings, I have felt a special affection for this beautiful metal, if one *can* feel affection for the inanimate ! How far we wandered and how many ladders we descended and ascended I cannot say. We remained underground for about two hours. The weight of the rocky roof was at many points crushing down the wooden props between which we made our way. Frequently we came upon and passed quiet groups of miners at work getting out the cinnabar, which was conveyed by small trolleys to the foot of a vertical shaft which we ultimately reached. I purposely say 'quiet groups' for there was something noticeably subdued about these men. It was with a sense of relief from the oppression of the darkness, the hot air and the risks of a fall into the unknown, that I finally stepped into the electric lift which was to take us to daylight. We ascended with a group of homeward-returning miners and stepped out into the open air far from our place of entry on the mountain side.

A torrential fall of rain was hammering on the power station and on all the buildings of the mines and village. The foaming Idrizza was thundering down its rocky gorge to the Izonzo and the Adriatic. There was still something of moment for my miner-guide to show me, *viz.* : the surface-workings lower down the river. At the risk of being 'amalgamated' with the Illyrian soil, we made our way

through the storm to some rather unsightly buildings on the edge of the village. Here were the
furnaces where the cinnabar is made to give up
its precious content. The spent ore, in the shape
of a whitish stone, or gangue, is poured into and
washed down by the foaming Idrizza. The furnaces are elaborate constructions heated by wood
from the surrounding forests or by producer-gas
obtained from wood. A small door was opened
for me in one of the ovens and I looked into the fiery
mass of incandescent cinnabar. The sulphurous
fumes and impregnated vapours made it difficult,
however, to linger in an atmosphere which the
workers apparently had become quite indifferent to.

From the central furnaces there emerged the
large cast-iron main by which the vaporized mercury is led away to the cooling and condensing
chambers of stoneware and wood. It must be
remembered that the average metallic content of
the ore does not exceed 1%. With volatilized
metal there passes off steam, soot and other matter,
and the retrieving of the mercury is a delicate
operation. For a brief moment a small trap-door
was opened for me in the main and the dense
bluey-grey fumes from the furnaces could be seen
slowly drifting past on their way to condensation.
I should imagine that the risks of mercury poisoning are greater here than in the mine below. Although my visit to Idria was a brief one, I heard
more than one account of the dangers of the
mercury-worker's life. The men die young, and
the village churchyard was close at hand to toll its
own sad tale. One miner I talked to had lost
most of his teeth : another was about to visit his
brother dying of mercury poisoning : and so on.

On the earthen floor of an adjoining shed were
ranged, penguin-like, scores and scores of the
mercury-filled iron jars, ready for the ox-waggon

and the outer world. I have said that each of these jars or 'flasks' as they are technically called, contains 76 lbs. of metal. They are closed at the top with iron stoppers which are screwed down tight by two men using a long lever. Thus stoppered, and without further packing, the mercury is sent upon its long journey. I was invited to lift one of the flasks from the floor : like a naughty child it seemed for a moment to possess the gift of non-liftability, but I was told that a miner thinks nothing of carrying two full flasks at a time suspended at each end of a short rod. In fact one of the men walked past me with two of the jars thus suspended. Some of the mercury is converted into vermilion, and I was shown specimens of this dazzingly beautiful product, which is in reality artificial cinnabar.

Many years have passed since William paid this visit to the Mercury Mines at Idria, and one cannot help wondering whether the Chapel, so movingly used by the miners to give them courage in their dangerous work, is still in existence, let alone used, in this rapidly increasing material world. William concludes:

The mines of Idria played an important part in the Great War, as the chief and almost only source of supply, of the mercury used by the Central Empires. A 'war communiqué' announced one morning that Italian airmen had crossed the Adriatic from Venice, and had distributed bombs on the electric power-station at Idria. If they really succeeded in their object, it is easy to understand that the destruction of the power-station would be a mortal blow which would lead to some furious thinking both in Berlin and Vienna.

I spent the night at the 'Schwarzer Adler' (the village inn) and never did I spend a night more comfortably. Electric light, clean sheets, and the best of food ! Being wet through, I had a hot bath and went straight to bed, and an excellent dinner was brought up to my bedroom. My hotel-bill, *tous frais payés*, and including breakfast the following morning, amounted to 4/- in all, a figure which led me at once to vow that I would one day come back again. At dawn I was awakened by the ringing of the church bells outside the bedroom window. Looking out on to the village square I could see emerging from the open church-door by the early light of dawn, what seemed to be the entire village of miners and their wives. This was simply a shift coming from prayers and going underground at break of day. In its simplicity there was something impressive in this devotion of these men returning to the duties and dangers of the mine. One felt that this was one of those scenes that must have come down unchanged from centuries past : a something that made me pause and think—this daily combination of faith and toil, repeated from generation to generation.

It was on the same holiday on the Continent that William Bellows had another unusual adventure, and he describes it:

I CAN see her still, the lustre of her beautiful hair caught by the light of the lamp upon the little table. I had visited the caverns of Adelsberg—surely the most glorious in the world—and emerging from their depths into the dazzling sunshine of a summer afternoon, with plenty of time upon my hands, had been advised by a resident to visit the Castle of Luegg, ' It is something you will never forget ' he explained. Accordingly by evening I found myself walking in a strange country intercepted by a barrier of mountains, with darkness settling on the land. I had set out upon my journey light of heart and light of luggage, my

impedimenta consisting only of a comb, a tooth-
brush, and a few spare coins for ready money.
But now the sun was sinking and I began to feel
concerned. What if darkness should overtake me
before I reached the village of Luegg ? In daylight this would be a strange world in any case,
but after nightfall, impossible. I struggled on and
the mountain range drew nearer. No soul within
sight or sound, no map to study, silence and the
deepening twilight ! At last the humble dwellings
of Luegg came into view, and there, overshadow-
ing the hamlet, rose the strange Castle still visible
against a background of rocky precipice. Another
mile or two and I stood in the silent village. The
sun had set. At this hour there could be no retreat-
ing. With puzzled step I at length found the village
inn. The landlady (for there was life here after
all) came out to examine rather than to greet the
stranger. I pleaded for a bed in a broken German
which she would hardly have understood if it had
not been broken. With difficulty I put it to her
that I must spend the night under her roof. No,
she could not accommodate me, she could not and
she would not. I continued the argument on her
doorstep, but steadily lost ground on account of the
language difficulty. What could I do ? Must I
sleep in the rough village street ? She ' could not
and she would not ! ' How awkward to have come
all this lonely way, to have brought my comb and
tooth-brush, and to find the door of the only inn
closed against me. And what an inn ! A grubby
place with a few small windows, yet how much it
stood for, and how my spirits fell when, with a long,
inward groan, I gave up the struggle.

Then, as if sent by heaven, there appeared an
angel on the scene ! Tripping down the grassy
slopes and leading a small boy by the hand, came
a beautiful young Croatian woman. She paused

and, coming quietly up to me, asked me in German if she could help me.

I explained my trouble and she began to discuss matters with the woman of the inn—in fact, to plead my cause. I listened in silence to the strange conversation as it ebbed and flowed. At last my angel-friend turned to me and explained that it was quite true that there was no bed available, for later that night there was to be a peasants' dance at the inn, and the landlady was helpless. But would I perhaps like to sleep at the Castle ? She could offer me no luxury, but would I mind the bare accommodation for otherwise she feared it would mean a night in the open air ! I gladly accepted her suggestion and we set out for the Castle. Before us towered the great barrier of rock which seemed to divide the known from an unknown world beyond. High up in the face of a limestone precipice, perched in the open mouth of a large cavern, rose the Schloss. In a gorge on our left there roared and foamed a river which, taking one final tempestuous plunge into the rocks below the castle walls, disappeared from sight, not to see daylight again for many miles. Threading our way in the dim light we came presently to the portcullis entrance. A huge and mouthy hound on a chain —I was thankful for the chain—received us with an awe-inspiring roar of welcome as we crossed the courtyard and ascended the great stone steps into the castle proper. Groping our way upwards by further steps and dim corridors we came at length to the living room of my young hostess. She was, in fact, the housekeeper of this cavern-fortress, her little boy her only friend and companion. Lighting an oil lamp she welcomed me to this plain chamber with its massive walls, its stove, its simple table on which she began to lay a meal, apologising for food, which, after those long miles,

159

proved irresistible. Besides ourselves there were here no other living beings but the hound below, and the bats, owls and such-like weird denizens of the all-embracing cavern. Outside, the night was dark and stormy : there were lightning flashes and the tumultuous roar of the disappearing river was silenced at times by the greater roar of thunder.

Our evening meal was over and cleared away and the little lad after following his mother in a simple prayer, had tossed for a while in his cot and was now asleep. Then as we sat in the lamplight with curtains drawn, my Croatian friend began to tell me her story—her sad life story. As she told it, her beautiful features with their exquisite framing of dark and lustrous hair, caught the reflections of the lamplight. In all my wanderings I have not seen a face more beautiful than hers ; the sadness of her story seemed but to increase its loveliness. Her father had been mayor of Agram (Zagreb), the capital of Croatia. She had married against his will and he had cut her off for ever. Then her husband died ; and now at the age of twenty-five she was a widow with this little boy of six as her only treasure—earning her livelihood at this remote castle, withdrawn from the world and from all her past life. Did she not find some companionship in the village ? No, the villagers were Slovenes and she was a Croatian ; moreover, what could she have in common with that ignorant peasantry ? Her great, her sole comfort was the little lad, now fast asleep, in whom all her lonely life now centred. The shadow of solitude was upon his life also, for he had no child companions. Whom did the castle belong to ? It belonged to Prince X, who sometimes came here for wolf-hunting with his friends. Never had she known an Englishman to spend a night here. From time to time she would peep in through a half-open door at the sleeping child. We talked till late into the night. My broken German, helped with sympathy and imagination, carried me along, but I could not say it all. I was deeply moved : to think that so much loveliness of life should be linked with life's frustration. Outside, the storm raged against the castle walls. The time came to light the candles. She led me up further steps and along corridors to the ' guest chamber ' of the castle : massive whitewashed walls, the simplest furniture and a window looking out upon the storm and darkness. The strange emotions of that hour and place ! ' Gute Nacht ' and ' Schlafen Sie wohl '—then ' Gute Nacht ' again and her steps died away into the depths. As the vision of beauty faded into the night, I was seized with a strange fear. I could but dive for safety into the bedclothes and blow out the candle. But I could not sleep. Where was I, in a real world or in a shadow world ? I lighted the strange tall candle again, jumped out of bed, and began to prospect. Opening a door, I peered into the gloom of the next chamber. With my candle raised aloft, I beheld a wolf gazing at me through the shadows, and then a bear, and further round another wolf and one or two more bears. I closed the door and fled with shaken nerves to the refuge of my bed. Torrential rain was falling outside and blinding flashes filled the bedroom and every cranny of the cavern-castle. Far below, the tempestuous river continued to plunge with its sullen everlasting roar into the unknown. At last I fell asleep. . . .

By degrees the light of a grey and stormy dawn filled my room. At the simple breakfast-table we renewed our talk. And then the sad moment came to bid her and her little boy farewell. It was difficult to leave. The Castle of Luegg had proved ' something not to be forgotten'. On my return

home she sent me some snowdrops from the mountain slopes and I sent her little boy some playthings.
And then the Great War came and overshadowed
all things.

It would have been interesting to have heard the other side of
this adventure – what it had meant to that lonely and sad young
mother, but there are not lacking other passages in the Continental
wanderings of William Bellows when 'the other side' *has* been able
to testify to the lasting impression left with them of the warm kindliness and encouragement which contact with him, however, fleet-
ing, had left behind it.

SCHLOSS LUEGG, POSTUMIA, NORTH ITALY

A COTSWOLD PROPOSAL

William Bellows and Grace Smith

(Self-taken)

CHAPTER XV

Late Romance and Marriage

HOW OFTEN MUST THE QUESTION have been asked, and still continue to be asked – how did William Bellows, with his universally acknowledged warmth of personality, his need of giving and receiving friendship, his altogether 'loveableness', how in the world could he still remain a bachelor till his middle sixties? It certainly puzzled, not to say concerned, his friends, the closest of them being well aware of a deep loneliness which he nevertheless managed to hide from most people.

The answer seems quite clear in the light of later events, for no matter what his need might be, he had the courage and wisdom not to be led into situations likely to lead to a fatal mistake. He preferred loneliness to anything less than a true marriage – nothing else would satisfy him.

In the light of all this, the story must be told as to how, and with apparent suddenness, the whole situation was changed.

A young widow with two small children, slowly recovering from the shock of her husband's fatal accident, was invited to a weekend house party by recently acquired friends in Rotherham, for she was living in the Peak District as her husband had taken up a post with a Sheffield firm. Being new to that district she had few friends in that part of England.

The house party was planned to enjoy what had by then become a time-honoured tradition, that is, to hear from William Bellows all he had to tell of his latest climbing holiday, and beautifully illustrated by his expert photography, projected on to the screen by his electric lantern.

It had often been remarked to her, 'Don't you know William Bellows? Haven't you met William Bellows?', to which she had to reply – well, she had vaguely heard him mentioned as his cousin and fellow climber had been a colleague of her late husband's, and their holidays in Austria and Switzerland came occasionally into the conversation.

The scene was set, preparations were shared in anticipation of an enjoyable week-end – coal fires lit in every bedroom, for was it not a coal-mining district?

She had agreed to help by printing the menus for dinner that first evening, and while doing so other guests arrived, including William Bellows. That meeting was as clear 45 years later as it was at the time, for it was a *recognition* – a recognition which could not be put into words but which was nevertheless undeniable. She felt vaguely surprised that *this* was the William Bellows she had heard so much about – well, of course, she knew *him!*

The die was now cast, but convention and decorum had to be served for they were two mature and responsible persons, each with a life full of unquestioned responsibilities. Therefore it was many weeks later that any further contact came about. He, with his load of commitments, and she, moving her home and children back to the south of England, and dealing with a sad accident to her son, mercifully then recovering.

So gradually events allowed of periodical meetings in London when he had to come to town on business, and she could arrange to leave her children, so thus they were able to become acquainted outwardly. It was a matter of most pleasant surprise to find that he belonged to Gloucester and the Cotteswolds, for there lay her own ancestral roots, and the district was well known and well loved. It all added to the strong link which they knew existed.

Correspondence then became the order of the day. Alas, that letter-writing has been largely pushed out of life in this present age of worshipping *speed*. So much can be conveyed in the written word which no convenience and time-saving of telephonic communication can entirely replace. It was a dignified way of confirming and enhancing a mutual awareness, but there was also a mutual willingness to let events take their natural course, controlling the inevitable outcome. There was never any need to hurry or press.

In a few months the way was quite clear, for no obstacles presented themselves, and so a future of close companionship seemed happily assured.

An invitation to use his Bungalow at Haresfield for the children's Whitsun holiday was more than welcome, not only for the change in a place of peace and beauty, but a golden opportunity for closer contact between William and the children, for they were thus able to accept the news of the change in their lives under ideal conditions, and welcome it, for they could not help already loving their future step-father.

William was happily able to visit Haresfield every afternoon, no doubt getting through his work at the printing works in record time! As the days went by he was able to bring various members of his family to meet this unknown future Mrs. William Bellows, for the stay in the bungalow was unexpectedly prolonged owing to the boy having developed measles. This proved to be a real blessing in disguise, for it gave them all a whole three weeks of comparative seclusion. Seclusion? Not exactly, for by that time the notice of the engagement had appeared in the Press, and telegrams poured in, so much so, that the post office in the tiny village 2½ miles away, asked permission to let a few accumulate before delivering, to save the long walk. The post-woman did not even have a bicycle!

What halcyon days those were! And preparing for a wedding no more than two months distant.

Never could there have been a greater output of correspondence, for Gloucester, not to speak of the wider circle of friends and relations, was not only astonished but delighted, and there seemed no end to the receiving and acknowledging of the wealth of congratulations. Then there were all the necessary preparations for what had to be a real public wedding for William's sake. It surely must be a source of amazement as to how much can be accomplished when there is unbounded joy in the doing of it! And most people must have experienced this at some time.

It was a miracle of achievement in every way – no one was forgotten, every detail given due attention, and no stone unturned to enable as many of his hosts of friends to attend the little village church at the Edge (seven miles or so from Gloucester) as that building could hold. Gloucester called it 'A Wedding of considerable local interest', and so it was, and much more widespread than just 'local'.

Perhaps a few typical extracts from some of the flood of congratulations will serve to show how much pleasure *William* gave to his friends in settling on his life's partner!

In spite of putting a formal notice of his engagement in *The Times*, William set out to inform his personal friends by writing a letter to each in his own hand. Those last few weeks before the wedding date, he kept a diary of all letters sent and received and noted other important items connected with the necessary preparations. It is therefore possible to record that he wrote no less than 120 of these letters telling each friend of his news, personally and individually.

The nature of the response to this mighty effort may be judged from the following passages chosen from some of these replies:

> We all most heartily congratulate you on your good news, which of course was a complete surprise to us, we having made up our minds long ago that you were a confirmed bachelor. Now things will all be changed with such a charming lady as you describe to be your life companion.
>
> from H. J. S., Purley, Surrey.

> My wife joins me in congratulations and good wishes and neither are conventional in any sense of the word. You deserve happiness in the fuller measure which marriage can bring. If I wrote at greater length I could not adequately express our feelings.
>
> May I however once more say how much we should deplore your relinquishment of public duties. We often differ, not as friends, and this exacting and thankless office leads one to value friendship.
>
> from T. W., Mayor of Gloucester.

> I will lose no time in congratulating you on the news H. has just given me, and on wishing you all happiness. Mrs. S. has been here more than once, and we all liked and admired her and are pleased she should be connected more closely with us. You will have no excuse for not bringing her here again! I can just fancy how you will love having a home quite of your own, and am sure it will be a lovely one. Let me have the privilege of

A CLIMBING HONEYMOON IN THE JULIAN ALPS, JUGOSLAVIA

WILLIAM BELLOWS
AS A FAMILY MAN

MR & MRS WILLIAM BELLOWS

cousinship, as well as of experience, and remind you that a woman likes to have her way in *little* things in the home, and can really judge of them best. She may be very amenable and complaisant – I should fancy in this case she is – but it is just then that noblesse oblige. What a joy the children will be to you, and what a help to her to have you!

from E. T., Newenden, Kent.

There can be no doubt that some of the letters raised a smile – but nevertheless feelings of gratitude for helpful intentions. The next letter, which has to be quoted in full, not to miss a single point, deserves to be framed since it was the one and only hint of any kind of disapproval, and is therefore unique!:

My dear and much respected Friend,

You must be puzzled that I have so long delayed in replying to the contents of your most extraordinary letter. It has been on my mind for patient consideration ever since. During the whole time I have known you, the one feature of your character has been the careful consideration of all things both great and small. And now to my great surprise I find you are about to embark on the most serious and lifelasting contract that it is possible for a man to make, and without any lengthened consideration, for as far as I can gather the time you have known your proposed partner is very short indeed. Now all the time I have known you, you have been your own master and could go anywhere you wished without let or hindrance, and so you have been able to live an interesting and useful life, both to yourself and to the community – as far I can judge. Now, under the proposed conditions all this will certainly be changed and you find certainly your ancient liberty encroached on in very many ways, and when this ecstatic condition which you call love has worn off, as it is bound to do – though you appear to have got a strong dose of it, more suitable to a boy than to a man of your age. Now the time will arrive when both parties must exercise patience, much patience towards each other, and all ought to be well. It is my most sincere hope that this will be so and that you will both enjoy the best of health and happiness throughout the remainder of your lives.

Again, my very best wishes, and I remain as ever your very sincere friend.   T. B. B., Welwyn, Herts.

To this William replied appreciatively of his friend's deep concern, and got this in response:

I am very glad to hear that you approve of my letter for I assure you that I gave more thought to your case than I have given to any event before.

It must be added here, that T.B.B. was the elderly friend whose Japanese collection William rescued from the Auction Rooms rather than let the treasures fall into strangers' hands.

So having dealt with the one note of disapproval (though it was accepted as a most sincere mark of true friendship), a few further extracts indicating overflowing approval follow:

Who said the age of miracles was past? Fancy W.B. falling a victim to cupid's arrow!

It is a bold venture but I knew you were not 'Faintheart' and from the negative you send the lady looks charming. At such a time, all I can do is to wish you all the happiness you wish yourself.

from J.S., Photographer, Whitehall, London.

Your letter this morning announcing your engagement to Mrs. G.S. and your marriage in the last week in July did indeed give me a thrill, and a delightful one too.

I hasten to send you both the heartiest congratulations of us all and our most sincere wishes for long life and good health to enjoy your happiness.

That's the truth and nothing but the truth – quite inadequate for this unique occasion. I should however be descending to mere journalese were I to put on record that you have, ahead of *The Times*, achieved your Everest (and that too might be interpreted as signifying that you have several times reached the 28,000 mark only to be rebuffed) or that, in future, lone unroped climbs will be but a reminiscence; so also the caption 'Bellows' last Blow', or 'Tuffley Dawns'.

So I will simply leave you peacefully to your bliss and beg of you to give us the earliest opportunity of meeting G. and of extending to her the same warm welcome to Hanlith as has been yours for so long, dear William.

from D.I., Kirkby Malham, Yorks.

Surprises never cease in this uncertain world! But I do congratulate you as I know what a charmingly dis-positioned girl you have chosen in G. I also like to think, and it amuses me to think, that I had some part to play indirectly in the affair. I shall be so interested to hear of your future arrangements. So you are planning the Julian Alps for the honeymoon.

from H.T., Newenden, Kent.

I can't tell you how glad we are to know you have found the true comrade for life. May you have the joy of one another for ever! some day you must bring her to see me and we must have a great talk. It is so wonderful when two people meant for one another find each other in this world. I am so glad you and she have.

from Mrs. W.D.B., Hilles, Glos.

Nothing could give me greater pleasure than to know that the supreme happiness is going to be yours, your letter was so absolutely genuine that it moved me to admiration of your heart – may I be at your wedding, my dear and good friend?

from Sir C.M.C., London

To say that the startling news in your letter surprised me is putting it very mildly, although I suppose nowa-days one should not be surprised about anything. However, please receive my heartiest congratulations on the important step you are going to take. Knowing how wise you are, I am sure you are doing the right thing and I wish you all the luck for the future that I am sure you deserve.

from E.C.M., Westminster, London.

The moment I opened your letter and that cheerful face greeted me at the breakfast table I knew what had happened without reading anything at all!

I know you made a wise choice and judging by the tone of your letter, there never could have been a happier couple! . . . Wonderful, what can all happen in so short a time!

from J.S. of U.S.A., travelling in Europe.

Well that *was* a surprise this morning when we got your invitation to your marriage! I hope to see Mrs. Bellows and yourself as invited guests here in St. Anna. Really, you could stay here some weeks instead of travelling over the whole continent as you used to do as a bachelor!

So, my dear Mr. Bellows, give us the pleasure to come here with the future Mrs. Bellows. You will get the finest room with bathroom, in the new house.

from Baron B., St. Anna, Jugoslavia.

You certainly have provided us with a real thrill, and I want to offer you my sincere congratulations. How you managed to remain a bachelor for so long I cannot imagine.

from C.T., (Business friend), London

Will you and Mrs. Bellows please accept my warmest congratulations on the occasion of your marriage, and my best wishes for your happiness. I feel that with the termination of your service on the City Council, the Library loses from that body one of its best friends and staunchest supporters. It seemed very appropriate indeed that in your final attendance you made a plea in connection with the matter connected with the Library.

I feel sure that although you have found it necessary to sever your connection with the Council, your understanding and kindly interest in our work will continue.

from D.W.B., City Librarian, Gloucester.

What amazing things are happening! Imagine my delight on receiving the card inviting me to witness your dive off the deep end!! My wife and I send heartiest wishes.

from D.W.H., Curator of Museum, Cheltenham.

Bless you! This is indeed happy news. All who hold you in affection, and how many they are, will rejoice in your happiness. Nothing can take the place of a woman's love for a man, or a man's love for a woman, and if you have waited longer than most, it should be all the sweeter to you.

from F.L., the Firm's Accountant, London.

I hear with pleasure and envy that you are receding from the Bachelor Ranks. I also hear that you are as happy as the day is long – well, I am choosing the Longest Day for my wishes. You may wish for, but Nature will not provide, a longer day! All happiness.

from A.B.S., Brookthorpe, Gloucester.

I have this morning heard the happy news that you are going to be married. Three cheers! Hearty congratulations – not only to you but to your future wife. Having known you for a long time and pretty intimately, I can safely congratulate her. And I am sure you will get on with the children – I am afraid you will be apt to spoil them, but it will be nice to have a ready-made family.

from Sir W.G., ex-Colonial Judge, London.

It was typical of William Bellows that for the five weeks or so of honeymoon, he would wish to share as much as possible of his favourite continental haunts with his wife. It was indeed a full, not to say an ambitious programme, and all meticulously worked out during those momentous pre-wedding days. All went to plan except for the big disappointment of the loss of a valuable camera, stolen, which meant great restraint over taking photos, always an important part of any holiday to him, and most especially this one. However, a very obliging Innkeeper in Bled, where the loss occurred, most kindly offered the use of his own camera. William had to make do therefore with a very inferior article, thereby reducing very considerably the number of pictures he would like to have

171

taken, and actually substituting picture post-cards for views which would be beyond the humble loaned camera.

In spite of this set-back, the tour was all that could be hoped for, and contained such an infinite variety of experiences quite fantastic to look back upon.

Starting out from Folkestone (his wife's birth-place, and marking therefore a second 'new beginning' in her life, then Basle, Villach, Bled, Trieste, and from there exploring Istria, containing such contrasts, e.g. Parenzo with marvellous pre-Christian Church and 4th-century mosaics, Pola noted for its Roman Amphitheatre! Inland, mostly on foot over sun-scorched arid country, hardly daring to sample the bed in the only Inn in Albona! Thence to the east coast and Laurana, as different from that in foliage and sophistication as can be imagined. Taking a small motor-boat across to a small uninhabited island, the water a clear pale green, was a refreshing episode indeed after the unbearable heat of Albona.

Visits to famous and breath-taking caves were included in the programme, Postumia (Adelsberg), already referred to in a previous chapter; now, since William's visit years before, become very much more sophisticated; but not so the caves at San Canzian where one had to depend on a small lantern carried by the guide, negotiating the ups and downs and ins and outs with great difficulty, and taking two solid hours to go through without retracing any steps. Such a relief to get into the open air and *light* after an awesome and unique experience.

Back to Bled as the starting-off point for climbing in the Julian Alps, but before that, paying the visit to Baron Born's Hunting Lodge Guest House near the Loibl Pass, which joins Austria and Jugoslavia. True to his word, the Baron, a picturesque figure in green velvet jacket and silver buttons, welcomed us as long lost friends and conducted us to the Bridal Suite! He is an Hungarian, and the wildness of the country, not to speak of the herd of wild Ibex roaming the hills, added a great sense of adventure and romance to the whole affair. Evidently, William was one of the Baron's most popular visitors. The woods stand out in the memory for the veritable *carpets* of wild cyclamen, pink and white. Surely the most superb of wild flowers!

172

One of the high-lights of this honeymoon was the sharing of a real climb – though Triglav, a mere 9,395 ft. can in no way be compared with William's Swiss Alpine climbs, yet it was an achievement for a beginner, and most enjoyable – sleeping in rough huts and meeting people of all nationalities and conditions.

Back to Bled once more, and this time, the last, going by way of the beautiful Vrata Valley, with wonderful falls, and the water everywhere a perfect clear onyx, to the next destination. This was the dignified home of Count and Countess Thurn, well known in diplomatic circles, and situated near Gustanj. It was through a mutual friend in Painswick in the Cotswolds that this visit came about.

Arriving after rough walking with no more than rucksacks, and so recently having made the ascent of Triglav, the clothes had naturally suffered and in some cases been torn, and otherwise *not* at their best. It was therefore rather humiliating to have them all taken away overnight by the servants, and returned almost 'as new'! To add to this, a suite had been put at their disposal – nothing so plebeian as *one* room, so they had to communicate through an open door, and with much suppressed laughter, note the coronets embroidered on all the articles of bed linen. This was indeed yet another level of experience on this amazing holiday!

The Count and Countess were courtesy itself, as one would expect, for they belonged to one of the oldest aristocratic families in Europe. But most sadly both son and daughter who were living with them, could neither hear nor speak. The son, a gifted sculptor, was longing to be accepted for study in the Paris Academy, and this William was able gladly to put in train for him. What happened when War came later is not known.

Steps were now turning towards home and in order to contact old American friends on holiday there, Wengen in Switzerland was visited. Later Geneva had to be included in order to meet a relative who lived there, and so completed this unforgettable 'sharing', and a fitting prelude to taking up the serious business of every day life, and getting adjusted to the many inevitable changes on both sides.

And so ended this romantic 'Interlude' in William Bellows' life, to be stored away in the memory as something very precious and a crowning to his many years of loneliness.

CHAPTER XVI

Visit to Nazi Germany
and Rescue of many Refugees

To ONE LIKE WILLIAM BELLOWS who had known and loved the mountainous regions of Austria, it was hard enough to endure the blight which had already settled over that lovely country, and which was sadly experienced in Innsbruck where a brief stop was included on the honeymoon journey – Swastikas dominated the scene, and an atmosphere of regimentation, so alien to the light-hearted Tyrolese, pervaded everything. The Nazi reign of terror had begun! But no one could then have envisaged what was to follow, and how the German people would allow themselves to sink to such depths of crimes against human life, expressed in the Pogroms against the Jews.

It has already been indicated that even before he contemplated marriage, William had decided to retire from his Aldermanship, and he felt himself even more entitled to a quieter life, now that he had a partner and a family to absorb him.

But it would seem that this newly acquired freedom did but release him for a far bigger task which lay ahead – a task which stretched his deeply rooted love for his fellows to the uttermost, and which took all that his great heart had to give of 'Love in Action'.

It happened that his wife, in the previous year, had met and been greatly impressed by a German lady, with some English blood, who had rescued her son from the Nazi Youth Movement, putting him to school in England where she could visit him from time to time. In the home where they met, the revelations of what private life in Berlin had become under Hitler made horrifying hearing, and included the plan for widespread domination which was clearly outlined in 'Mein Kampf'. To English ears it took on the nature of the fantastic dreams of a madman – but how mistaken we were in our complacency!

So when the world was rudely awakened to the goings on in Germany, and her wholesale persecution of the Jews, it seemed obvious to his wife that William should meet this German lady himself. Sitting back and expressing horror was not enough when cruelty stirred him.

This lady was about to return to Berlin after spending the summer holidays with her son, and straight away invited William to visit her in her home, and see for himself just what the situation really was, in Berlin and elsewhere.

But such a task must be prepared for – to go into any scene of disruption unequipped physically and spiritually does but add to the disruption, and inflict injury on the would-be rescuer, serving little purpose.

This is where William manifested his natural wisdom, so his visit to Germany was prefaced by a short, but telling few days in his beloved Swiss Alps, using every opportunity for ski-ing and solitary mountain walks. He knew in his soul what it was he had to face, and that it was up to him to go equipped. He now had the solace and outlet of sharing with his wife, and though family responsibilities prevented her from accompanying him on his Mission of Mercy, letters flowed to and fro, giving her as accurate a description of the situation as he dared.

It was perhaps unfortunate that a young Jewess he had known in Gloucester as an 'au pair' girl to some friends, should have caught up with him in Switzerland, for she had recently escaped from Berlin, but very anxious for her brother's safety there. Naturally, she was all too ready to fill his ears with first-hand and horrifying information as to the prevailing conditions there, and could well have undermined his purpose in letting Switzerland strengthen his defences for the work on hand. He had, very gently but firmly, to explain things to her, and was therefore able to keep matters under control. He said afterwards that it had at least served the purpose of breaking some of the ground before actually reaching Berlin. Each case of human anxiety and despair could so easily sap the energy needed for a larger service, and it only goes to show how priceless is the quality of true wisdom which enables its possessor to exercise sympathy and help without undue loss or wastage by the way.

Just a few days sufficed, through the untiring activity and direction of his hostess, to put him in touch with this one and that one, desperate to escape from Germany and needing sponsorship. Relief Committees, like the Quaker organisation, were contacted, and although official channels had to be used for permits to leave the country, William made himself personally responsible for 11 people, which did not include their wives and children.

During those days in Berlin William wrote to his wife:

> . . . Early morning, sitting up in bed before being called by our friend who is always so brave, so patient, so heroic. I have unbounded admiration for her. Further contacts yesterday, including D's brother. He comes this morning at 9.
>
> Today is *their* great day, not ours. Flags everywhere, miles of bunting – like the Pass above Baron Born's, but a thousand fold. I was never in touch with suffering on so vast a scale. If it was not my duty to be here I could not stand it. The memory of winter sports has faded into insignificance. Compared with this, what is it? The tragedies, the tragedies – the broken lives – the despair!
> . . . Carry on, darling, I'm soon coming back, but I had better finish – this is such a responsibility – human lives
> . . . A tap at the door then, our brave friend announcing 8 o'clock.
>
> Berlin is a city of great distances. Except for the brave heroic ones, it seems to have no soul. One has to come here to understand this peculiar soul-less quality. . . . Our friend is well and sends her love. I am so comfortable with her. I am doing good work – but oh, so busy. It is impossible to write here as we can at home. I can explain later. All goes well, but so much business in so short a time.
>
> A day of further difficult interviews and efforts. This has been no holiday here, darling, but I am a *thousand* times glad of the privilege and great responsibility of having been able to come here. . . . My hostess, as you know, is a perfect dear and a heroine; always smiling – always *so* selfless – faced at every turn with immense

difficulties – a life of supreme devotion and self-sacrifice. The world little knows the beauty of her character. I cannot tell you how unbounded is my admiration for her. She has been a tower of strength to me and such a perfect hostess. It is through you, dearest, that I have come to know one of the very finest women I ever met. She and I spent two hours on Tuesday with the President of the Jewish Community of the German Reich. I have had some quite wonderful contacts since coming here. This city is like a huge semi-American city that has lost its soul. Something seems to have dropped out of it.

Oh, I cannot begin to tell you everything. Our friend and I go down into the centre of the city this A.M. after receiving our second visitor today. The streets are plastered with what we saw fluttering in the breeze near the borders of Jugoslavia. . . . Am learning much. Dear love to little G. *Here* she would be enrolled! [G. aged 8].

Back in England William began the task which he had undertaken in promising sponsorship. But first, he felt impelled to make known to the community at large, and his friends in particular, the enormity of the Nazi crimes, and the need not only to welcome persecuted ones into their homes (domestic help was in great request) but to try and understand what these poor souls had suffered – indignities and cruelties quite unknown, mercifully, in this country. For this purpose, he and his wife invited many to attend meetings in their home, when William steeled himself to recount some of the many grievous experiences that had come to him.

A recent letter from U.S.A. to his widow told of an incident during William's visit to Germany, entirely unknown to her till then. It reads:

What I still remember about his stay in Frankfurt is the most valuable experience he gained on his way to see the S. family, whom he had never met before. He went there unannounced, and when my sister-in-law opened the door and saw a complete stranger asking for her husband, she naturally expected him to be coming to take her husband to the Concentration Camp!

177

This gave her such a shock that she fainted! This was the best demonstration your husband could get to convince him about the urgency for his rescue work. How selflessly and successfully he worked for this cause is a story that will never be forgotten, and for which we will all remember him as the great human being he was!

So now came the up-hill and discouraging task of getting official permits from the Foreign Office to allow his protegées to come to England pending permits to enter the U.S.A. or elsewhere, according to opportunities open. How William suffered from the frustration of red tape – a dossier at the Foreign Office could be (and many were) overlooked and held up, but when it meant a human life at stake, he could be a real fighter against Bureaucracy. Those were indeed anxious days, involving many a journey to London before they were safely in England. One couple was sent to Lisbon before they were able to get over to America, but it was William who made it possible for them to find safety. This doctor (he was allowed to follow his profession in U.S.A.) wrote later to William's widow:

> We, and so many other emigrants lost with Mr. Bellows the best friend and kindest helper. We never will forget that only his unprecedented generosity enabled us to leave the hells of Germany and to find in this happy country the possibility to rebuild a new life. In this difficult way we found many helpful people, but none of them can be compared with our best and most unselfish friend, our dear Mr. Bellows.
>
> We will never forget him and always will deplore that this benefactor could not live to see the final victory of the decent people.

It was no easy task absorbing this little company of refugees and finding accommodation and so on. Two married couples were housed up at Haresfield in that Bungalow, already made quite notorious for one reason and another. Although simple and lacking many amenities, the peace and safety of it helped to restore their flagging spirits, and they were within visiting distance moreover.

Another family found a home with one of the Printing Works 'widows', and the children were accepted temporarily at the local school.

It would be almost impossible to give full details. One couple found a home in Birmingham and their daughter, a brilliant girl, was given a place in Roedean School. An achievement even William could not help being proud of, for she did him very great credit and was also fortunate in finding a lovely family in the Cotswolds to provide a home in the school holidays.

This same girl, who with her parents have remained most loyal friends these 40 years and more, writes as follows:

As one makes one's path through life, one pauses at times to reflect upon the past and the persons and events which helped shape one's development. Whenever I thus contemplate, I feel duly blessed that I had the good fortune to meet Mr. Bellows, and to have been privileged to have his guidance, help and advice at a time when everything seemed to fall apart, and all values, as I had known them, were ruthlessly destroyed. He not only, through his sincere interest and devotion to all those in distress, revived my faith in humanity and life as such, but he in particular also had an everlasting influence upon the path I was to follow from there on. He was a unique human being who had the gift to immerse himself totally into the problems of others, with the sole purpose of trying to solve those problems, alleviate any pain and restore happiness and peace of mind.

He made it possible for me to have the best education and to experience life at such an outstanding school as Roedean. To this day – 40 years later – I am again and again reminded of the solid foundations to my education that were laid there, and upon which I could build ever since. He also steered me to a profession in which I found great satisfaction and happiness.

In summing up, I can only state that the memories of my contact with Mr. Bellows, of our conversations and correspondence, are amongst my most cherished possessions.

In some ways it might seem that constant repetition of the same theme is superfluous, and yet the fact that recognition of William Bellows' deep caring for his fellow creatures comes from such a variety

179

of sources cannot but underline the truth that goodness one to another sets in motion an influence that can be far more outreaching than can be imagined. Would that the press and similar organisations would give more prominence to that which would encourage and uplift mankind, instead of the daily dose of horrors and sensationalism which all too often fill our newspapers.

One of William's Jewish protegés was a Doctor of Law from Vienna who had lost his wife and child in horrifying circumstances and although he had desired to be sent to America where he had a brother already established there, he was directed to Australia where he knew no one, and made to do manual work in some Camp. He chose cobbling. Never did a word of complaint pass his lips; he worked hard, and in time was allowed to qualify himself as an accountant. Since then he is happily re-married and retired. A regular contact by letter has been kept all the years since, and he wrote recently recalling his first meeting with William:

> It happens in a person's existence sometimes that he meets a man whose personality enriches the rest of his life. Such a man was William Bellows whose memory I treasure.
>
> I met Mr. Bellows who, a perfect stranger to me at this time, had sponsored my stay in England, in June 1939. I came as a refugee from Nazi persecution to London after my release from the German concentration camp at Dachau. Apart from the material support there was Mr. Bellows' kind personality which helped me to overcome my heavy depressions caused by the separation from my family and the progress of the War in the first years. When Mr. Bellows came to London on business he always found time to talk with me and thus to alleviate my distress. After more than 40 years and being in the eighties, I do not remember the words he used – I admired his language – but I remember very well the effect. I finally acquired a serene outlook on life.
>
> I would like to mention that I spent an unforgettable week-end at Mr. Bellows' home in Gloucester and met Mrs. Bellows who, I am sure, played also an important part in Mr. Bellows' field of charity.

When I was in Gloucester, I met two couples whom Mr. Bellows had helped to come to England from Germany, and I remember the director of the Relief Committee in London praising Mr. Bellows as one of the most generous friends of the oppressed and persecuted.

This was my great experience of meeting Mr. William Bellows.

from Dr. L., Melbourne, Australia.

What a wealth of undying appreciation William drew just as the result of his simple acts of kindness which were as natural to him as breathing. It surely is a comforting thought that there must be many 'William Bellows' in the world, and though their deeds go unrecorded, yet the effect of those deeds lives on in the hearts of men for ever. The power of good is an emination of the Power of God, and must and will triumph over ALL – eventually.

CHAPTER XVII

Last Tributes from Friends

THAT WILLIAM BELLOWS failed to reach his three score years and ten could be called a tragedy, but which of us could claim to know *how* long a life should be? That he made the very fullest use of his span of life has been clearly shown in these pages, and perhaps was able to put more into the years allotted to him than many who even live to make their century.

The Dean of Gloucester, who gave the oration at William's committal service, expressed it most beautifully, he said:

> The departure of William Bellows made the community immeasurably the poorer. He lived in the plenitude of his rich years, before the limitations and weaknesses of old age diminished his powers of body or mind.
>
> He inherited an honoured name, and he maintained the lustre of that name.
>
> He would be remembered with gratitude in the literary and cultural circles, certainly in three continents.
>
> But it was not so much of his public and professional life that they desired to remind themselves, but of his personal character and goodness. The good William Bellows did in the community would live long after all of them had passed away. They thought of him as friend and as a good Christian man.

What better way to complete the story these pages have tried to tell, than by handing it over to others, for it is only by the fruits of his service that a man can truly be known, and their lasting value established. Effortless goodness needs no name or label, it speaks for itself. Like true music, which is inspired, it goes on living for posterity and its influence is therefore boundless:

I was shocked and deeply grieved to see the notice in *The Times* today.

William was one whose friendship I greatly valued. One could speak freely with him. His unyielding tenacity in holding, and his inflexible purpose in pursuing what he believed to be right were bound with a truly charming sense of fun and a delicate whimsical humour.

In discussions he showed the greatest interest in the views of others, and made clear an anxiety to learn from all, often from those he was in a position to teach much.

As you know, we used to meet occasionally for an interchange of views and experiences in the field of printing, and I recall the confession he made in several of our earlier talks that he suffered from a sense of loneliness – no brother or other one, as I had, to share anxieties. This sense of loneliness was very real and very sad. I think you may like to know how, on his marriage, he left it quite behind. Never again was it spoken of to me . . .

I am President of the South Western Alliance of Master Printers, and while this little note is written as a friend of William's, I would express too the sense of loss which will be felt throughout our area by Master Printers who appreciated his craftsmanship, his leadership, his faith and his wide interests and sympathies.

A holiday with W.B. was something of an adventure because we seldom knew exactly where we were going and never booked rooms ahead. He assumed a carefree, joyous spirit and was out to make the most of every minute. This coupled with a fund of whimsical stories and an ability to talk well on almost any subject, made him an ideal companion. It was his making the most of every minute that always made me sigh with relief when, rucksack on back we were tramping up some valley towards the high places having left trains far behind. He never appeared to hurry, rather the reverse, and I had many anxious moments swallowing a last mouthful in a station refreshment room, with our train waiting several sets of rails away and probably a subway to traverse – W.B., watch in hand saying;

'Why hurry, there's half a minute yet!' I cannot recall that we ever missed a train.

William Bellows, printer, publisher, French scholar, photographer, Alpine climber, friend of the Cotteswolds, friend of the down-trodden wherever he found them, friend of writers in every land – how many a tie far and near must have been severed by his death, how many unknown friends must join us in saluting his memory. There was hardly a corner of Europe in which William Bellows could not count on a welcome, often from someone to whose family he had done a kindness many years before. He had friends among men of letters in every capital.

Especially close were his ties with France, many of them inherited from his father and cultivated by him during his constant visits to that country, either in connection with his work on his Anglo-French Dictionary – also a pious heritage – or for pleasure. Small wonder that with these qualifications he was invited to work at the Ministry of Propaganda during the last War, where he collaborated with such men as John Buchan, Ian Hay, Henry Newbolt and Edmund Gosse. His friendship with the last named continued until the day of Gosse's death. Many a journey did the two take together in England and in France, and Bellows loved to tell his friends of his experiences. Indeed it was characteristic of him that he loved talking of all his experiences, and very good talks they were, often illustrated by those wonderful photographs which he seemed to have an uncanny instinct for taking at exactly the appropriate moment. Few men ever used their camera to better purpose or produced more beautiful work.

Bellows was a good fighter in spite of his Quaker blood – perhaps that was the reason for his worship of Napoleon. Of his courage there was little doubt. Did he not start mountaineering when well over 50, and twice climb the Matterhorn, on the last occasion making the traverse from Zermatt to Italy and the descent in a howling gale.

In the last year or two before the present war he became increasingly absorbed in the work of bringing help to the victims of Nazi persecution. Cruelty always stirred Bellows to a white heat, and the Nazi regime filled him with loathing. At a time when many respectable people were carefully stopping their ears to the cries of anguish that came to us from across the water, and when many English magistrates were punctiliously returning to their torturers prisoners who had escaped from Dachau, Bellows was running grave risks in visiting Germany, in establishing relations with the Jewish community there, in organising the escape of individuals and was helping them on this side with his means and sympathy. All honour to him.

That William Bellows had innumerable friends was inevitable. His kindness, his generosity were boundless. His whole life was given up to helping others.

Perhaps one of his most marked qualities was his delightful sense of humour – of fun, and his disarming simplicity.

It was always such a pleasure to see him and exchange thoughts and views on so many things which interested us both. I do not dare to think of what the loss must be to you, but it will truly be shared by his many friends who will miss him sorely. One felt he was one of the few people one could go to with confidence for advice or help in any difficulty. Forgive me for talking so much about one's own sorrow, but it only makes me realise more what it must mean to you, and hope you will accept all my deepest sympathy.

The loss of my old and very dear friend is a bitter blow to me, but how terribly hard it must be for you . . .

If ever there was a good man it was William. I had known him intimately for 25 years, and through all the ups and downs of life he was always the same cheerful, encouraging and helpful friend. I can never forget the innumerable things he did for me, and how his sympathy and affection helped me through a very sad period of my life. His great circle of friends prove what I say, and I know of many kind acts, so quietly and modestly done, which helped many a poor struggling soul.

No doubt he must have told you of the many adventures and delightful excursions we had up and down the country. Of all my friends I know of no one with whom I could be happier, and his wide knowledge of the world, literature and humanity was a constant stimulant to me, as it must have been to others.

And then you came into his life and gave him the greatest happiness a man could want. So often when an old friend marries one is liable to drift away, but not in this case, and your kindness and affection for his old friend touched me deeply. I loved my visits to hospitable Tuffley Lawn, and you were both always so welcome here, and we loved having you.

I can't say more, my heart is too full of sadness, but I do want you to know how much I feel the loss of one of my oldest and dearest friends, and how my prayers go out to you that you may be given courage and strength at this moment and in the future.

I know we shall always preserve our love, respect and admiration for a really good man whose life was not in vain.

And so we will leave these tributes with these words which came from a Master Musician:

"Both in public and private life there will be many who will miss that vivid personality – so eager for knowledge, so valiant for truth, so tireless in well-doing.

But great as these qualities were, it was his wonderful sense of humour, with its odd comparisons and whimsical allusions which made him so companionable.

It is a great and comforting thought that one can say that no one ever came in contact with him who was not the better for the friendship."

JOHN BELLOWS *m* ELIZABETH EARNSHAW
1831-1902   1841-1932

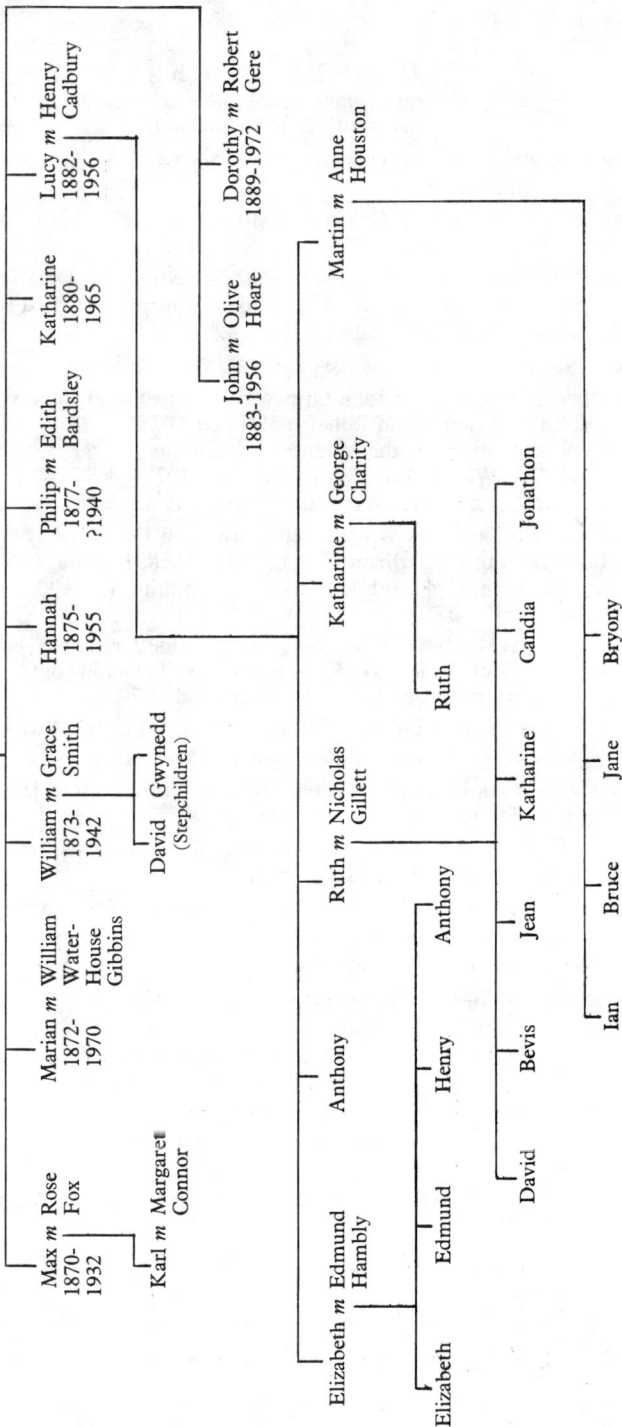

Max *m* Rose
1870-   Fox
1932

Karl *m* Margaret
      Connor

Marian *m* William
1872-   Water-
1970   House
      Gibbins

William *m* Grace
1873-   Smith
1942

David   Gwynedd
(Stepchildren)

Hannah
1875-
1955

Philip *m* Edith
1877-   Bardsley
?1940

Katharine
1880-
1965

Lucy *m* Henry
1882-   Cadbury
1956

Dorothy *m* Robert
1889-1972   Gere

John *m* Olive
1883-1956   Hoare

Martin *m* Anne
     Houston

Elizabeth *m* Edmund
      Hambly

Anthony

Ruth *m* Nicholas
    Gillett

Katharine *m* George
      Charity

Elizabeth

Edmund

Henry

Anthony

David

Bevis

Jean

Katharine

Ian

Bruce

Jane

Candia

Bryony

Jonathon

Ruth

Compiled by David Smith, the author's son.

QUAKER BOOKS
available from Quaker Bookshops or direct from
Sessions of York, England

THE BEGINNINGS OF QUAKERISM (to about 1660) — The Standard work by Wm. C. Braithwaite.

THE SECOND PERIOD OF QUAKERISM (to about 1725) also by Wm. C. Braithwaite. Reprinted 1979.

BARCLAY'S APOLOGY in modern English — edited by Dean Freiday. Reprint 1980. This statement of Quaker principles was first issued in Latin in 1676 and in English in 1678.

QUAKERS: their story and message, by A. Neave Brayshaw.

QUAKER ENCOUNTERS by John Ormerod Greenwood in three volumes
Vol. I   Friends and Relief (published 1975)
Vol. II   Vines on the Mountains (published 1977)
Vol. III Whispers of Truth (published 1978)
A history series on Quaker relief, missionary and overseas service.

NO CROSS NO CROWN by William Penn with a new Foreword by Professor Hugh Barbour of Earlham College, Richmond, Indiana, U.S.A. Reprint of the 1682 edition, also incorporating the 1930 edition's introduction.

THE FRIENDS MEETING HOUSE by Hubert Lidbetter, FRIBA. Historical Survey of Friends' places of Worship from the beginning of Quakerism including plans and photographs. Reprinted 1979.

LAUGHTER IN QUAKER GREY and MORE QUAKER LAUGHTER. Two volumes by William H. Sessions of humorous Quaker anecdotes.

FRIENDS IN YORK by Stephen Allott. The Quaker Story from 1651 in the life of a Meeting.

THE TUKES OF YORK. Presented by W. K. & E. M. Sessions. Narrative of the well-known York Quaker Family.

JOSEPH ROWNTREE 1836-1925: A Quaker Businessman by Anne Vernon.

SOMERSET ANTHOLOGY by Roger Clark. 24 pieces written for the Village Essay Society of Street, Somerset — edited by Percy A. Lovell.

A HISTORY OF SHOE MAKING IN STREET, SOMERSET: C. and J. Clark, 1833-1903, by G. B. Sutton.

LUKE HOWARD 1772-1864. His correspondence with Goethe and his continental journey of 1816. Edited with commentary by Emeritus Professor D. F. S. Scott.

ENERGY UNBOUND by Kenneth C. Barnes. The history of Wennington School.

WILLIAM FRYER HARVEY 1885-1937: A Friend with a Difference, by Rev. C. E. J. Fryer.

CAROLINE FOX 1819-1871: Quaker Blue stocking of Plymouth: Friend of John Stuart Mill and Thomas Carlyle, by Robert Tod.

WOODBROOKE 1953-1978: The 3rd 25 years by F. Ralph Barlow, edited by David B. Gray.